Economic Minorities in
Manpower Development

Economic Minorities in Manpower Development

Eloy R. Mestre
State University College
Oneonta, New York

Heath Lexington Books
D.C. Heath and Company
Lexington, Massachusetts
Toronto   London

Copyright © 1971 by D.C. Heath and Company

Published simultaneously in Canada.

Printed in the United States of America.

International Standard Book Number: 0-669-75994-5

Library of Congress Catalog Card Number: 71-170634

To Eva, Ricardo, and Sandra

Table of Contents

viii

List of Tables

Acknowledgments

Acknowledging my intellectual and moral debt to those who have helped me in one way or another is a gratifying but difficult task, because it is always hard to find the right words to express one's complete sense of gratitude.

First, the greatest debt of all; and mine is to my wife, Eva, for her continuous and unfailing encouragement. She, my children and my family have all given me the moral support necessary to the completion of this, or any, undertaking.

The development of a person's ideas is most certainly influenced by his intellectual and professional interaction with his colleagues and mentors. They cannot be held responsible for one's intellectual errors or one's views, but they do share in whatever contribution one might be able to make. I want to express my appreciation for the support and assistance of the colleagues with whom I have been privileged to work, particularly those in the Economics Department of S.U.C.O. Especially, I want to thank Dr. Sanford D. Gordon, chairman of the department, for his understanding and guidance, and Alfred M. Lubell, my office-mate for the past four years, who has assisted me so much personally, and in my professional development.

I wish also to acknowledge my immeasurable debt to my professors at the New School for Social Research, for their contribution to my professional and intellectual growth, but very especially for the kind of education they gave me. Likewise, I want to thank my professors at the University of Havana.

I also want to thank Mrs. Evelyn Katrak for her editorial work, and Mrs. Sue DeJoy and Mrs. Beth Brower for their secretarial assistance. Their time and patience is very much appreciated.

Thanks are due, too, to the State University of New York Research Foundation for partially supporting this effort.

Last, but by no means least, a very special thanks to all those Cuban nationals who so generously assisted me in my field work. My appreciation also goes to those agencies and groups working with Cuban national refugees for their kind cooperation.

Introduction

The issues of manpower development, poverty and income maintenance have been receiving considerable attention in academic and political circles. They already occupy an important place in the literature. At stake is the very continuance of a way of life. These issues have not always been placed, however, in a proper analytical perspective; for they are not separate phenomena, but rather aspects of the same problem—namely how to conquer economic insecurity.

The role of manpower development in an overall economic security strategy that can facilitate the efficient performance of free markets within the framework of an advanced industrial environment that permits maximum individual freedom seems to be an important and timely subject for inquiry. This study represents a modest attempt to place this problem in a better analytical framework compatible with the American value system.

The objective of the study is threefold. First, it is concerned with an analysis of manpower development in general, and an examination of its role with particular reference to the American economy. At a more specific level, the objective is to examine the potential of manpower development in assisting economic minorities to improve their absolute and relative position in the American socio-economic structure, and to explore how much consideration thus far has been given to the plight of economic minorities in the designing of manpower development strategies in the United States. The third objective is to explore the potential of labor mobility and resettlement programs as a major manpower development weapon in the struggle against poverty in the United States. In this connection, field work conducted on one such program—the resettlement program for Cuban National Refugees—is discussed.

The study is presented in two parts. In Part I, some important issues raised in the study of manpower development within the above stated analytical framework are discussed: 1) changes in the structure of the American economy that have made the subject important; 2) the role of manpower development in a free market economy; 3) the relationship between manpower development and the level of economic activity; 4) manpower development as part of the wider issue of economic security; 5) the role of manpower development in assisting economic minorities; 6) legislative effort in the manpower development field with particular reference to the problem of economic minorities and the establishment of a comprehensive manpower development strategy; and 7) summary and outlook for the 1970s.

Part II, a study of mobility and relocation programs as part of this nation's manpower development policies, is divided into four chapters: 1) an introductory discussion on the importance of labor mobility in a market economy and the extent of labor mobility in the United States; 2) an examination of current efforts to develop mobility programs in the United States; 3) a detailed discussion of the resettlement program for Cuban National Refugees; and 4) a concluding summary to the second part. (The methodology used in the field work in this final section is explained in the introduction to that section.)

Manpower development is the main link between human resource conservation and the labor market. It is not a new concept, having been an object of discussion in the economic literature, in one form or another, for many years. But the term itself is rather recent. The term "manpower development" defies any precise definition. In general, it includes anything that contributes to an increase in the productivity of labor and to the more effective employment and deployment of the labor force. Manpower development policies, then, refer to those policies concerned with the attainment of these objectives.

The decade of the 1960s witnessed the prelude to what might prove to be a profound revolution in the American socio-economic system. Never before have the American people seen so much legislation enacted in this field, touching on almost every aspect of manpower: area redevelopment, vocational education, higher education, rehabilitation of the poor, etc. The major thrust in the manpower development field, at least in principle, came during the latter part of the decade with passage of the Amendment to the Social Security Act. Calling for the training and employment of all recipients of public assistance over the age of 16 unless specifically exempted, this Amendment represents a landmark in manpower development policy in the United States. In addition, Congress and the Administration have been actively searching for new means to supplement and/or maintain income for those with inadequate incomes or with no income at all. The possible passage of the Manpower Revenue Sharing Act, the minimum income proposed by President Nixon, and further strengthening of the Social Security program are likely to provide a new thrust during the 1970s and move this nation a step closer to having a comprehensive economic security strategy.

The beginning of a new decade seems an appropriate time to evaluate and reassess the knowledge gained from experiments carried out in the manpower development field during the preceding decade. As F.M. Hechinger has suggested: "Next to defeat a revolution ought to fear victory most."[1]

It seems safe to state that manpower development has become one of the major issues in the American economy. It has joined full employment, price stability, rapid economic growth, and improvement in the quality of life as one of the major goals of this country. Most relevant is that manpower development has turned out to be pivotal to the attainment of these other goals—a point that will be elaborated upon later in this study.

Amid this profound transformation, one thing remains unclear. To what extent has the social and economic rehabilitation of economic minorities been the primary target of the manpower development revolution that has been taking place in the United States? The problems raised by this question are discussed extensively in this study. However, it should be pointed out here that the relevance of this question lies in the fact that the social and economic evolution of this country can be seriously hampered by the existence of a sizeable number of people to whom the term "economic minority" applies. In the absence of adequate means to provide a minimum of economic insecurity, any major change in the structure of the economy may swell its ranks considerably in the foreseeable future. Manpower development is one very important avenue open to this society to effect the incorporation of economic minorities into the mainstream of American life and provide, at least in part, this minimum of economic security that is so necessary to the very existence of the American way of life. Manpower development offers an opportunity to accomplish this within the general framework of traditionally accepted values.

At this point it is necessary to explain the meaning of the term "economic minority" as it is used in this study. The terms "minority" and "disadvantaged" are often used interchangeably in the literature. Moreover, they are usually associated with poverty. It is rather obvious that not all minority groups are disadvantaged, and vice versa, but there is an overlapping. Any group of people which, for one reason or another, becomes impoverished over a protracted period of time tends to acquire the social status of minority for its members are precluded from sharing in the prosperity enjoyed by the nation as a whole. The very fact that the incidence of poverty[a] seems to be declining renders such groups of people an "economic minority." The use of this term seems preferable on the grounds that it facilitates the extension of the analysis made in this study to any group of people in this country who are precluded from effective participation in the market, regardless of what factors may have brought this about.

---

[a]If the concept of poverty bands is used, it is possible that while the proportion of people living below a minimum subsistence level may have declined the proportion of those living below minimum adequacy (or even minimum comfort) but above minimum subsistence may have increased.[2]

**Part I:
Manpower Development and
the American Economy**

1

The Dynamic Nature of the American Economic Process

In this section some of the major changes that have occurred, or are expected to occur, in the American economy and that should have an important bearing upon manpower development analysis and policy, will be examined. Although most of these changes are relevant to manpower development in general, they seem especially to affect economic minorities as will be discussed in the course of the first part of this study.

In a stationary economy, namely one where the variables comprising the system, the value of the parameters and the institutional framework do not change significantly, major disruptions in the functioning of the system should be a rare occurrence. Under these conditions, the demarcation line between active and passive manpower development policies is almost non-existent. In a dynamic economy, on the other hand, one or more of the factors comprising the system are subject to change; economic readjustment is necessitated whether this is government induced or just natural process; and sometimes the system is smooth and rather predictable but most of the time it is not. When this happens, the system's variables are constantly thrown out of line with one another. Usually, though not always, they bring concomitant changes in the institutional framework. It is then that the constant readjustments required can be quite painful economically, socially and politically speaking.

The American economy seems to be a vivid example of this pattern of economic and social change. Under these conditions, a sharp distinction has to be made between active and passive manpower development policies. The former can play a vital role in bringing some order into this state of affairs, particularly in reducing the heavy burden that rapid and continuous economic change imposes on individuals. This becomes a must where discriminatory practices are applied to certain groups since the burden then may become intolerable for those groups.

Changes in the size and composition of the population are at the heart of manpower development analysis. They are among the most important variables affecting the economic system, for they can affect both the size and composition of aggregate demand and supply. In the American case they seem to have been among the most dynamic variables. Table A-1 in the appendix shows past and projected changes in the population in the United States.[a] Under the intermediate fertility assumption the projected increase in population between 1970 and 1990 is larger in absolute terms than the one that took place between 1950 and 1970. The projected increase for those two decades combined is

---

[a]All tables with an A letter can be found in the appendix.

approximately 60 million people. In relative terms, the population is expected to increase at about the same rate as during the 1960s, namely between 13 percent and 15 percent per decade. This is somewhat below the record high 1950s. Even if the low fertility assumption were to materialize, the projected increase would still be approximately 43 to 45 million people—equal to a medium-sized nation. This increase in population is subject to considerable variation on a year to year basis; that is, the impact on the labor and product market is likely to be uneven.

There are two aspects of the composition of the population that are very important in devising manpower development policies; they are age composition and racial composition. Table A-1 shows the major changes that have occurred in the age composition of the population between 1950 and 1970 and those that are anticipated between 1970 and 1990. Take, for example, the age group 20 to 24 which affects the labor market so crucially. From a decline of 4.8 percent during the 1950s it increased during the 1960s by 54.5 percent, it is expected to rise by 21.7 percent during the 1970s and then decline during the decade of the 1980s. On the other hand, the very productive 35 to 44 age group is expected to increase by 11 percent and 44 percent during the current and next decade.

The racial composition of a growing population should pose no special manpower problem if it were not for the legacy, and one which still persists, of discriminatory practices. The fact is that non-white groups are a very important and special component of the economic minority family. The increase in the non-white population over 16 years of age was 24 percent for the 1960s and has been projected at 26 percent for the current decade.[1] The corresponding figures for whites are 15 percent and 5 percent, respectively. Particularly worth noting is the increase of over 50 percent that took place among non-whites, ages 16 to 24, during the 1960s and which is expected to be over 30 percent during the 1970s. These figures lend support to the concern with the manpower development of economic minorities. They also suggest a very important factor behind the civil rights movement, although that issue is a much broader one.

It appears then that the challenge posed by a very rapid increase in population, and in its composition, to this country's effort to improve its human resource base is still very much with us. If anything it promises to become even more severe because of the present backlog of things left undone in this regard.

Population seems to be the most important variable affecting the size of the labor force; however, it has long been recognized that this association is not one of proportionality. Between 1950 and 1970 the American labor force grew from 63.8 million workers to 85.9 million workers, an increase of approximately 22 million people (see table A-2). By 1985 the labor force is expected to comprise 107 million workers. This represents an additional increase (1970-1985) of 21 million workers. It is expected that 8 of the 21 million additional workers will be women. This is quite a different story from what took place between 1950 and 1970 when 13 of the 22 million workers that were added were women. This suggests a slowdown of the very rapid increase in women's labor force participation that has occurred since World War II.

Table A-2 also shows considerable changes in the relative contribution made by each major age group to the total labor force, from one decade to another. Though it is true that changes in the age composition of the population have some bearing on this, there have also been significant changes in the pattern of entry and exit of married women as affecting the age distribution of the labor force; for example, decisions to have children early in the marriage play a role here.

The significance of population and labor force growth in the establishment of manpower development policies goes well beyond what the above might have already suggested. For example, natural increases in population are not likely to match increases in jobs on a regional basis—even assuming that the distribution of skills is ideal. It was seen before that non-whites have exhibited a well above average rate of increase in population; the same goes for people living in rural areas. Considerable evidence exists, however, that jobs have not been rising at an above average rate in areas where these two groups are predominant, that is, farms and central cities.

Table A-4 suggests that the growth in population and labor force which occurred during the 1960s and is expected to occur during the 1970s, varies considerably from one region to another. For example, it was as high as 30.1 percent in the Mountain region and as low as 8 percent in the West North Central. All this suggests that either people or jobs will have to move; otherwise regional differences in unemployment rates will develop which may be difficult to correct. Complicating this problem, though independent of it, is that the labor force participation of non-whites (a very important factor in this study) has increased relatively faster than that of whites, a trend that is expected to continue during the 1970s.[2] This suggests that the matching of jobs and workers for this group is quite a challenge, as the American people have already begun to realize.

Another dimension of the population variable which has been subject to considerable change is life expectancy. This is significant for manpower development policy because changes in this variable can influence the allocation of time in regard to work, leisure, and skill development (i.e., education). Professor Seymour L. Wolfbein, who has probed into this matter using data for 1900 to 1960, has found, for example, that a group of 100,000 boys born alive under today's conditions will work, on the average, about one million more man-years than they would have worked under 1900 conditions; yet, they are likely to enter into the labor force later, work fewer days a year with a shorter work week, and even afford to retire younger.[3] This is a dimension of the labor force which has often been neglected, but which has affected the American economy profoundly.

Another aspect of work that has undergone some change is voluntary part-time employment. During the 1950s, the number of persons over 14 years of age working voluntary part-time schedules doubled (in 1957 it was approximately 100,000). This number has remained rather stable throughout the 1960s. However, the actual number of part-time jobs is likely to be much larger than the above figure indicates, for it does not include people working part-time schedules for economic reasons. These are people that would like full-time employment but are unable to find it. Throughout the 1960s the number of people working part-time for economic reasons fluctuated around the 2 million mark; however, it must be borne in mind that many of these jobs represent reduced work schedules rather than true part-time jobs. At any rate, if those working part-time schedules were to find full-time employment, they would release jobs for those who are only able and/or willing to work if they can find part-time employment. No doubt changes in the occupational-industrial structure of employment has contributed to this rise in part-time employment; for example, the growth of the service industries where this sort of employment is easier to arrange. Automation has certainly played a role in this development too; however, it is likely that increased automation blurs the line between full-time and part-time work as workers demand more leisure, particularly in the form of a shorter work-week. Table A-5 shows the age groups that have taken the greatest advantage of this kind of employment are the 18-24 male group and the 25-44 female group. This suggests that any future increase here may help young people who want to work while attending school and married women, particularly those raising a family.

A problem not unrelated to the above issue is that of multiple job-holding. The development of new opportunities for part-time employment coupled with a shorter work-week may be encouraging more people to take on two or more jobs at the same time. Contributing to this possibility is also the rise in professional employment where part-time assignments are not difficult to create. Between 1956 and 1970, the percentage of those employed holding more than one job was approximately 5 percent to 6 percent.[4] In view of the increase in total employment during this period, this suggests an increase of close to 1 million people in this category. This aspect of the labor supply is not likely to remain unchanged during the 1970s and, therefore, should also have some bearing upon manpower development.

The quality of the labor force is another important factor which has proved to be quite dynamic. More and more, the idea of investment in human beings in the form of skill development has been recognized, and a considerable amount of research is currently underway in an attempt to reckon its contribution to economic growth.[5] This is particularly important since the average person has more time to invest in the development of his skills, and also has more time to reap the benefits from such an investment, too. Table A-6 shows a marked increase in the median number of school years completed for persons 18 years and older between 1940 and 1970. Future gains here are expected to be, on the average, more moderate in view of the high level already attained. The most significant development in this respect seems to be the very noticeable narrowing of the gap in average educational attainment between whites and non-whites, particularly in the case of males. If the past trend continues non-whites, especially rural residents, should show the greatest gains for there is still plenty of room left here for improvement. This is a critical problem for economic minorities.

Although the median number of school years attained seems to be a reasonably good proxy for the quality of the work force, at least as a first approximation, the gains suggested by it underestimate seriously the actual improvement in the quality of the labor force, as Professor T.W. Schultz has so clearly explained.[6] In the first place, it does not take into account the length of the school year which, on the average, has been increasing. It does not consider differences in one year of schooling between young and old workers, nor in the quality of the education received. This is a thorny problem; for older workers, who find themselves having to look for jobs, are forced to compete with younger workers who are, on the average, much better equipped educationally, particularly since most of the new jobs do seem to require a higher quality of education. On all of the above accounts then, median number of school years underestimate the gains in quality experienced by the American labor force. This factor, though understood, has usually been neglected in the designing of manpower policies.

Thus far evidence has been introduced on some of the major changes affecting the size and composition of the American labor force; however, in the designing of a manpower development strategy, an appreciation of the fundamental changes taking place on the demand side are crucial, too. The fact is that these two phenomena are so closely interrelated that one cannot be adequately perceived without understanding the other.

Gross National Product (GNP) increased in constant dollars (1958 prices) from $203.6 billion in 1929 to $724.3 billion in 1970.[7] It has more than doubled since 1950 alone. This represents an average annual rate of growth of between 2.5 percent and 3.5 percent, a rate of growth which is expected to be at least maintained during the 1970s. Success or failure in our manpower programs could be the difference between an above or below average rate of expansion during the current decade. Gains in employment, however, have been more moderate than the rate of growth in production (approximately 1.5 percent per year on the average) because of the tremendous gains in productivity experienced by the American economy; for example, between 1947 and 1970 the index of output per man-hour for the private economy rose from 51.3 to 104.6; however, the most remarkable achievement in this respect can be found in the farm sector where the index rose from 29.2 in 1947 to 113.1 in 1970.[8] This, by itself, would have necessitated a considerable amount of adjustment in the economy.

Interesting as these figures are, they do not reveal the magnitude of the change involved, for the composition of that increase in production was profoundly altered throughout this period. Changes in income, family size, age composition of the population, place of residence and the like have changed the consumption pattern of the population. This, in turn, has resulted in considerable variation in the rate of growth of the various sectors of the economy. Table A-8 shows evidence of the major changes that have taken place in the distribution of personal consumption expenditures. The major change has been the relative decline of the demand for non-durable goods, particularly food-related items and the marked relative increase in the demand for services. No drastic changes are anticipated in the current pattern of consumption expenditures by major industry groups during the 1970s. This, of course, conceals variations in intragroup composition and in quality.

The distribution of employment is affected not only by changes in the composition of aggregate demand, but also by intersectoral variations in productivity gains; for example, a given sector may be experiencing a very rapid increase in demand for its product, but gains in productivity may suffice to satisfy it. By the same token, an industry may have experienced only a moderate increase in demand not accompanied by a parallel increase in productivity. This industry may then become an important source of additional jobs. Table A-9 shows the very large interindustry variations that have existed, and that are likely to exist, in the average rate of change in domestic output. This alone is capable of keeping the American economy in a constant state of flux.

In line with this argument, some of the sectors exhibiting the most rapid rate of expansion in production, like the communications and public utilities sectors, have also posted some of the largest gains in labor productivity, therefore providing relatively few new employment opportunities.[9] Other industries, like the service ones, have shown very substantial gains in demand for their product accompanied by an enlargement of their employment base, since gains in productivity in these industries have been, on the average, relatively small. In other industries, the gains in productivity have been so large relative to the increase in demand that jobs have been lost. This has been the case in agriculture and mining.

All this suggests that intersectoral differences in the expansion of demand on the one hand and of productivity gains on the other, go a long way in explaining the present occupational and industrial structure of the American labor force.

As the evidence in tables A-10 and A-11 shows, this structure has experienced a very profound change over the past two decades and is expected to undergo still further changes in the foreseeable future. The present occupational and industrial structure shows a clear pattern of increased dependence on employment expansion in the service industries and in the government sector, with particular emphasis on white collar and service type occupations. Even in those sectors where employment has remained rather stable, or shown only moderate increases, there has been a significant change in its composition; the trend has been toward a very large relative increase in white collar employment and a significant relative decline in blue collar employment. This appears to have been the experience of the manufacturing, public utility, and transportation sectors. It reflects, to a large extent, the introduction of automated production processes.

In the non-agricultural sector, white collar employment has risen from about 37 percent in 1950 to 48 percent in 1970, and it is expected to go as high as 50 percent by the end of the current decade. However, even this group has undergone considerable change in its composition. The major gains have been reported among professional and technical jobs and, to some extent, clerical type jobs. The composition of the white collar occupational category is likely to be the most affected by further developments in automation in the years to come. Blue collar occupations, on the other hand, have been losing ground steadily, except for the craftsmen group which, on the average, has been able to hold its own. The service occupations, other than household work, have reported substantial gains as a result of the very rapid expansion of this sector. Farming, of course, has been hit with the largest losses in employment.

The effects of automation are far from clear; while some sectors of the economy are just beginning to be affected others are already in an advanced stage of automation. This is important because different stages of automation seem to have different types of labor requirements, while the latter, in turn, is influenced by the availability and quality of the labor supply. The fact that automation is here to stay is suggested by the increased willingness of unions to accommodate to it.[10]

To all these changes in the occupational and industrial structure of the labor force changes in location should be added. One of the most dynamic aspects of the American economic development has been the location of industry.[11] Since different industries have different location patterns, it stands to reason that interindustry differences in the rate of growth are bound to affect the geographic distribution of employment, and indeed they have.

One of the best indices of how painful this continuous process of change could be, and of how unevenly it may affect different groups, is probably the unemployment rate. It points to incomplete or inadequate readjustment on the part of the economic system. Table A-12 strongly suggests that relatively high average rates of unemployment have persisted since 1950. It is clear that the unemployment rates have been, and still are, highest for the youngest workers and to a somewhat lesser extent for workers over 55 years of age. Regardless of the age group, non-white workers have exhibited much higher unemployment rates than their white counterparts. This situation has become particularly acute among young, non-white workers, especially teenagers who have dropped out of school. Also worth noting is that the unemployment rates for women have tended to be somewhat higher than for men, particularly during the 1960s. Since younger workers (especially non-whites) and women have been the major contributors to the growth of the labor force over the past 20 years, the above development concerning unemployment rates suggests some serious difficulties in absorbing this kind of labor into the labor market.

Table A-13 shows that the unemployment rates have been persistently much higher among blue collar and service workers than among white collar ones. This has been particularly true among unskilled workers. This development is not unrelated to the relatively large increase in the supply of this type of labor; i.e., women and non-white young workers. However, it also reflects the relative decline in the demand for this kind of labor and the fact that newly created jobs usually require new and better skills.

Concerning the persistence of high rates of unemployment during the last two decades, it should be pointed out that during the second half of the 1950s and early 1960s long term unemployment (15 weeks and over) hit a record high (25 percent to 30 percent of all unemployment).[12] This was particularly true of those unemployed for over 27 weeks. There seems to have been some correspondence between the above development and an increase in the rate at which automation was being introduced in American industry, for the latter adversely affected the growth of production employment.[13] This also accounts, at least in part, for the heavy unemployment among low skilled workers. Finally, since economic change has not affected all regions to the same extent, the incidence of unemployment has been very unevenly distributed on a regional basis, as table A-14 suggests. Also, considerable intercity variation in unemployment rate has existed throughout the past two decades. In some cities, unemployment rates have been as high as 12 percent (Johnstown, Pa., for example, in 1960). Even during the very rapid economic expansion between 1965 and 1968 unemployment rates of over 7 percent were not unknown in some cities.

The incidence of unemployment is likely to have been much greater than the unemployment rate figures suggest. It was noted earlier that part-time employment for economic reasons has fluctuated around the 2 million mark for quite some time. This, and the difficulties inherent in measuring underemployment, strongly supports the view that unemployment rates seriously underestimate the extent of unemployment in the United States. The major significance of this shortcoming in accounting for all unemployment is that most of this underestimation concerns economic minorities. This, combined with the existing above average rates of unemployment for groups where economic minorities are highly represented, particularly in the long term category, suggests that the incidence of unemployment has been, on the average, much greater for this group, and that manpower development, as a means of alleviating the burden of economic readjustment, is of even greater urgency for this group.

Thus far, nothing has been said about institutional factors and, admittedly, they could bring about change, not only as a force in themselves but also in reaction to changes in the major variables of the system. The list of such changes in the American economy could be quite impressive, therefore only a few examples will be mentioned here: child labor legislation, changes in international trade agreements, the development of the Social Security system, the growth of organized labor and, of course, wars. All of them have left their mark on the economic system. One of the most significant developments, however, is the expansion of urban life which has brought about profound changes in our social framework.

It seems clear then that the American economy has been subject to very profound structural changes that do cause very serious dislocations. Also, that these changes are likely to continue in the foreseeable future, and if anything, the tempo of change may be gaining a new momentum whose consequences are difficult to discern. Moreover, it is clear that while these changes place some burden on society at large, above all, they place a very heavy burden on those directly affected. At times they mean upgrading, at other times downgrading;

frequently migration has to be resorted to, as well. This may happen to an individual several times between his entry into the labor force and his exit from it. All this is usually accompanied by demands on the individual to change his life-style and his personal as well as his family relations. This strongly suggests the powerful role that an adequate manpower development policy can play in helping the economy to readjust with a maximum of ease and a minimum of social friction.

If this country wants to reap the benefits of these rapid economic changes it might have to find ways of distributing the burden of change on a somewhat more even basis. A program of manpower development is a partial answer to this challenge. As the above analysis strongly suggests, the process of adjustment has, in the past, placed a much heavier burden on economic minorities than on any other group. (However, it should be emphasized that this is partially due to factors like housing and job discrimination, less opportunity to invest in their own skill development, etc., factors that find no justification in the process of economic change). As will become apparent in the course of this study, manpower development for the economic minorities is, therefore, a very complex, but also a very vital issue.

2 Manpower Development in a Market Economy

The purpose of this section is to examine the meaning and possible role of manpower development in a predominantly market-oriented economy. This is relevant because manpower development has to be carried out within the framework of a given economic system. Its analysis cannot be conducted in an institutional vacuum. Manpower development policies that might contribute to a better utilization of available labor resources in one type of economic system with its particular institutional framework may prove of little value when applied to another type, and vice versa. This is an often forgotten consideration when manpower development policies that seem to have been successful in one country are recommended for use in another without proper qualification.

The American economy still is predominantly a market economy; hence, it is of paramount significance to comprehend the meaning of manpower development in this kind of economic organization if it is to play a meaningful role in facilitating adjustment to economic change. This is particularly important if economic minorities are to be aided within the present framework of accepted values, and if the intention is to incorporate them into it at the earliest possible date.

Before proceeding, however, there is one central question to ponder: why, at a time like this, when many people, either by their actions or their failure to act, appear to have lost faith in such a form of economic organization, will this study examine manpower development within this very frame of reference? Isn't this simply being obdurate? After all, the market system itself is blamed, in part, for many of this nation's ills. Why then is there not an attempt to discuss the potentiality of this weapon within a different economic framework? In reply, it is important to note first that current efforts and policies in this field still have to be carried out in an economy that relies principally on the market mechanism, and any appraisal of these policies cannot ignore this. Second, it is believed that many of this country's problems exist not because of the market system, but in spite of it, or because it has not been permitted to function properly. Finally, in the hypothetical sense, it is precisely an adequate manpower development strategy that can contribute most to the effective working of this form of economic organization under conditions of constant change.

In the designing of manpower development strategies, reference is frequently made to manpower planning; this requires clarification, however, in its application to a market-oriented economy. The term economic planning is generally viewed as the antithesis of free market economics and indeed, in its purest form, it is. Manpower planning is a central aspect of general economic planning. This

13

suggests, then, the possibility that manpower planning may turn out to be but a subtle way of introducing economic planning into the system. It can be manipulated as to make it a first step in this direction. No wonder it has been resisted by people in this country who fear economic planning and see it in fundamental conflict with the basic principles of a free market economy. These fears should not be dismissed lightly even though they may appear somewhat unfounded at times, particularly since this country has evolved, by mutual consent, into a "mixed" economic system. However, a "mixed" economic system is in itself a concept that is fraught with ambiguity; it can mean anything from some government participation in the economic process to a rather high degree of control by government, as the American and European experiences suggest.

Students familiar with the recent work of Professors Robert L. Heilbroner and John K. Galbraith will surely recognize the possibility of using some sectoral planning as a means of laying down the foundations of further economic planning. Of particular interest in this connection is their belief that the American economy has been increasingly subject to private economic planning, a trend they seem to believe will continue and is profoundly modifying this country's political and economic structure. Particularly Galbraith sees in technology the roots of this development, for it is difficult to raise the very large sums of capital required for production under modern technological conditions unless it is possible to secure ahead of time a share of the market. For this reason, he sees no harm in the growth of oligopolies and of the modern corporation—usually a conglomerate.[1] It might be surprising that two writers who supposedly have different views could independently have developed similar arguments; however, the economic mechanics of controlled economies, regardless of what specific subgroup does the controlling, do not seem to differ significantly from one variation to another whether this be economic corporatism, socialism, or any other form. Unfortunately, any extensive discussion of this issue is beyond the scope of this study.

That the American economy is moving in the above direction there seems to be little doubt, although the dynamic nature of the economy and the non-monolithic character of the major power groups in the system may have served to slow down the above process. For example, the farming and labor blocks are comprised of groups that do not always have the same interests or share the same views. That this trend is good, as Galbraith suggests, or that this trend cannot be stopped or even reversed regardless of how people feel about it, or that it is basically due to modern technology, are entirely separate issues subject to serious questioning. Admittedly, some minimum form of planning might prove necessary; for example, there has to be a certain minimum degree of educational planning. But an effort should be made to refrain from deliberately influencing the outcome, except to the extent that it reflects predominant cultural values. Also, during the evolutionary period on the way to an economy that will provide equal access to economic opportunity for all, a need might exist to influence the workings of the system, but only to bring those left out into the mainstream of American life. If some form of planning is to be used in the American economy it is very important then to be able to distinguish between planning that interferes with the market process—or even tries to supercede it—and planning that attempts to make the market mechanism function more nearly optimally; that is, it should assist in validating the allocation of resources intended by the free interaction of the market forces, and not one dictated merely by the preferences of a powerful few.

In an economic system which satisfies all the criteria for perfect competition, planning of any kind is irrelevant and redundant. The perfect competitive market has built into it its own form of planning—the so-called "invisible hand"—which is not the meaning of planning as used in the economic literature. There seems to be no need to elaborate here on the obvious, namely that the American economy has never functioned in this way. The United States economy is full of market imperfections: unions, oligopolies, minimum wage constraints, licensing, and social and economic discrimination are but a few of its major manifestations.[a] It should be clear, however, that the presence of market imperfections does not mean that a market does not exist. This simple point has led many people to misunderstand the working of a competitive economy. Manpower development, as a limited form of manpower planning, can serve to correct and/or offset some of these imperfections. This is another role of manpower development in a market-oriented economy, for some of the imperfections that exist in the American economy have become largely institutionalized and are here to stay since many of them reflect the needs of an advanced industrial society; for example, collective labor negotiations whereby group conflict becomes institutionalized.

A very real danger exists, however, that in the effort to correct certain market imperfections new ones might be added. The idea of countervailing power for which Galbraith has been given credit, is rather, an example of one imperfection failing to offset another, serving only to suffocate the system.[b] It is unfortunate that it is so hard to draw a hard and fast line between these two types of manpower development policies: the countervailing and the effectively corrective. This accounts in part for the present state of confusion regarding the feasibility and possible effect of various alternative approaches to the manpower development needs of this country.

As a rule, but not always, corrective manpower development policies such as those designed to increase labor productivity (regardless of who is involved), to make labor more mobile in response to changing economic conditions, to spread information on labor market conditions, to make employable workers out of

---

[a]An evaluation of the extent of free competition in the American economy is beyond the scope of this work.

[b]This is the case where increasing the power of unions was expected to offset the market power of employers, where the latter have had considerable power. But when different or opposing groups have similar power, the corporate state is approximate which indeed, in its most advanced form, supercedes the market system.

unemployable ones, to reduce bottlenecks and market frictions, to end discrimination and, in general, to create an environment of equal opportunity, are not in conflict with the basic tenets of a free market under conditions of rapid change. In general, they tend to make the labor force and labor market more responsive to the constant state of flux of the economy at large. In principle, the fundamental test is that the performance of the labor market in allocating scarce economic resources efficiently be improved, with benefits exceeding costs. This, of course, is more easily said than brought about; however, these principles ought to be kept in mind when drafting manpower development strategies in this country.

The projection of labor market requirements by occupation, industry, region, etc. for a given period of time—usually a rather long one—has recently become fasionable.[2] On the surface they are just projections; however, deep down they reflect employment planning, particularly of the private sector. This strongly suggests they might be serving as instruments of sectoral manpower planning. The more private enterprise and/or the government can control production and markets, the more they can anticipate their labor requirements since they will also be able to influence the rate at which they want to introduce new methods of production. The underlying assumption seems to be that by making these projections the supply of labor would adjust to the demand for labor as suggested. They might encourage present and would-be members of the labor force to respond in such a way as to maintain market equilibrium with a minimum of friction and wage-salary adjustment. This is thought to be important because training and retraining are time-consuming processes which might cause serious bottlenecks in production. This desire for manpower forecasting to support production planning has stemmed in part from fears concerning the disruptive nature (for the labor market) of rapid technological change. Yet, it is this rapid technological change and its dynamics that are most likely to contribute to making these projections of very limited value because it tends to change production functions, thus affecting the skill content of the labor input required to produce a given output.

The most serious problem that manpower forecasting appears already to be posing is through its influence on the planning of this nation's educational output. Admittedly, it is hard to say to what extent our educational output has been so influenced, but that it has been so affected seems undeniable. One may wonder if there is not a contradiction here considering some of the projections used in the preceding section. In the first place, some of the variables discussed there represent, at least in large part, a datum to the economist, since they do not depend on economic forces alone. Second, as long as this nation's policies tend to validate those projections and the public to respond to them, they will tend to materialize; for this reason, in a study of this nature, they cannot be ignored under present conditions.

Any student of market economics knows that when the market mechanism is allowed to function with a minimum of inteference, the demand for and supply of the various factors of production determine their relative price. Relative price, in turn, determines, to a very considerable extent the proportion in which the factors of production are combined. In this connection, various grades of labor can be thought of as different factors of production. It is obvious then that by generating a given output of the various grades of labor (based on a given set of manpower projections) it is possible to alter their relative price, hence encouraging employers to adjust their production functions to the new set of relative prices. Moreover, by altering factor proportions and relative prices, it is possible to influence the pattern of technological change; for the relative profitability of alternative means of production is also bound to be affected by such a policy—that is, these variables are interrelated. To the extent that some of these projections are based on the expected needs of producers and/or the government, who also know, at least to some degree, their plans to introduce technological changes, their intentions become validated in the process. All this suggests that this form of subtle planning has no useful role to play in a well-oiled, market-oriented economy. At least, it points to its futility.

An important question still remains unanswerd: how is it possible that this type of planning is often said to be capable of improving the performance of the market economy? This apparent confusion seems to have its origin in at least two theories. First, that employers very seldom resort to adjustments in factor proportions in response to changes in relative prices.[3] Most economists would agree, however, that these adjustments in factor proportions are a rather common occurrence in the American economy. The fallacy of this theory seems to reside in the failure to see that adjustments in factor proportions can take many different forms. They are not confined to capital-labor substitution, though this takes place, too. Factors such as changes in techniques of production, organization of work flows, and more or less supervision are some alternative ways of obtaining similar results.

The second theory centers around the idea that the very advanced technology that is being introduced in the U.S. and the new industrial state accompanying it are imposing private planning as a byproduct on the American people. Some of those who hold this view see the market sector as having to operate under this new constraint; therefore, manpower planning, if only in the limited form of manpower forecasting, might be the only way of maintaining the efficiency of the labor market in allocating scarce economic resources. One major problem is that the resulting trend towards still bigger business, labor, government, etc. has been contributing to the erosion of whatever is left of the market system once the above technological constraint is introduced into the system. In this connnection, it is worth pointing out that much of the legislation enacted during the past 60 or 70 years in the areas of business, labor, and related fields, and particularly the way in which the courts have tended to interpret it, has been responsible, to a significant degree, for the partial breakdown of the market mechanism as the chief method of allocating scarce economic resources in the United States.[c]

Through these legislative and judicial processes scores of market imperfections have been either tolerated or introduced into the economic system and, in turn, these have greatly facilitated the growth of big business, big labor, etc. This attitude has not always been related to the introduction of technological change. The underlying assumption behind this general behavior seems to have been more one of providing countervailing power and protecting special group interest than of facilitating the working of a free market. Whether this past development is reversible or not depends in large measure on the political process and the general attitude of the American people and not so much, as might be thought, on the economic one. A commitment to make the market mechanism work is necessary if it is going to be workable. With adequate legislative and judicial support the market system cannot only be made more competitive, but it can also be given a greater role in the economy as a whole. It is extremely dangerous to assume that private ownership of the means of production insures automatically the existence of competitive markets. It is unfortunate that many advocates of a competitive market system have failed—or do not want to see—this simple point and, as a result, are not inclined to take steps to reverse this trend at the political level.

The strongest case so far for this kind of undercover manpower planning in a market economy is that quite often the adjustment of labor supply to changes in labor demand has been rather slow and time-consuming. Of course, this is a relative matter and it depends considerably, as further discussion will indicate, on whether or not there exists adequate means to help people caught in the transitional process. The intersectoral transfer of labor tends to be difficult in a technologically advanced economy due to the high degree of skill specificity that tends to exist.[d] The result is that wages and salaries tend to rise in sectors where labor shortages occur. This would pose no major problem if it were not for the fact that these wage and salary increases are difficult to reverse once the

---

[c]A few examples seem to be in order, unfortunately, a detailed account of this legislative development is far beyond the scope of this work. Antitrust legislation was passed, but later the positive effect that the passage of this legislation might have had upon competition was, at least partially, offset by legislation protecting monopolistic practices (e.g., the Fair Trade Act). Moreover, competition has been controlled in the area of farming, but most of the benefits have accrued to the owners of large farms. Tariffs and tax policies seem mostly to have benefited large enterprises. The state legislatures have also had an ambivalent attitude concerning these problems. The courts have quite often changed the intention of the law; this has been especially true in the area of antitrust where sometimes monopolistic practices have been endorsed de facto. Currently, it is possible to witness the reluctance of both the courts and Congress to take any action against the growth of conglomerate mergers. Perhaps one of the greatest sources of power for big business have been the Patent laws governing this country. They have been greatly abused and are by now outmoded.

[d]Although this line of argument has some points of contact with the theory discussed above, it is not the same. Here, it is not necessary to insist that technological progress is dictating production planning.

adjustment has been completed; manpower planning has something to recommend it when it can help to reduce this problem.

It is interesting to note that this is just another way of saying that labor markets are imperfect. In this connection, two things have already been suggested. First, that many of these imperfections have been introduced via the legislative-judicial mechanism. Second, that manpower development can be used effectively to offset and/or eliminate these imperfections.

There is another argument which applies primarily to the educational aspect of manpower planning. It is conceivable the American people might have come to accept that the provision of a maximum amount of education from which a person can benefit is a desirable long-range goal in itself, to be pursued regardless of its impact on the labor market (benefits being measured not only in monetary terms). In this event, education would have to be viewed much more for its possible value as a consumption service and other national objectives than for its possible effect on the functioning of the labor market. Socio-cultural values take precedence here. The major implication of any such policy is that the labor market would have to operate within a kind of socially dictated framework. If there were no further interference with the labor market, however, relative factor prices would adjust to this new framework and would tend to reflect the effect of this group decision concerning education. This is a possibility which should not be dismissed too lightly, for this kind of long term social goal may be gaining acceptance in the United States; for example, witness the tremendous growth in public and subsidized private education. This is an instance where the institutional framework influences the operation of market forces.

The prime objective of this section is to establish that not all kinds of manpower development policies can be applied to a predominantly market-oriented economy without coming into conflict with it. But also, that in a market full of imperfections manpower development policies can be of great value. The use of manpower development policies that are compatible with the principles of the market system to aid economic minorities has sometimes been questioned. As far as this author is concerned, this ought to pose no insurmountable obstacle for the existence of economic minorities is in large measure the result of market imperfections past and/or present and, therefore, manpower development policies designed to correct this situation are well within the limits of tolerance of a market economy. This is an issue that will be examined in some detail in Chapter 5.

The underlying philosophy of this study is then that manpower development in the United States, whether for economic minorities or not, should be geared to the optimization of the performance of the market system, the latter being constrained only by the values imposed by the American cultural setting.

3 Manpower Development and the Level of Economic Activity

This section focuses on the relationship of manpower development and the level of economic activity—an attempt to bring the analysis started in the preceding section into a somewhat more specific context; that is, to consider how manpower development can help to improve the performance of the economy at different levels of economic activity.

The analysis presented here has a twofold objective: first, to examine the pivotal role of manpower development in maintaining a more nearly balanced economy where the cost of trade-offs among the major objectives will be greatly reduced; and second, to explore the problem of manpower development in an economy confronted with various types of unemployment. These two aspects of the relationship between manpower development and the level of economic activity are not entirely independent analytically, but a deeper insight into that relationship is likely to emerge from discussing them separately.

Manpower development is a continuous process—as is the process of change in the economic system—however, its nature tends to change with the level of economic activity. It is a misconception to think that manpower development is something to be implemented only during periods of widespread unemployment and recession. There is no question that manpower development can be of great value during such periods; as a matter of fact, in an economic system that is mixed in nature and full of market imperfections manpower development can be very effective in mitigating the effects of declines in the level of economic activity and, therefore, rendering this process less disturbing. But assisting unemployed workers to find jobs by various means is only one aspect of manpower development.

This attitude towards manpower development seems to derive from two factors: first, a very narrow and emergency-oriented type conception of manpower development whereby it is associated largely with unemployment; second, the fact that a great many of the manpower development policies inaugurated during the early 1960s were primarily addressed to the problems of the unemployed. Actually, to some degree the latter reflects the former, but it also reflects standard congressional behavior whereby most issues are considered to be of a short-term and transient nature. Not only are periods of unemployment and recession the time when people are most inclined to look into the value of manpower development, but they are also the time when the opportunity cost to society of using manpower development weapons might appear to be relatively lowest, since the contribution of these workers to production is nil. This however is a rather short-run interpretation of oppor-

21

tunity cost. If the average productivity of unemployed workers is increased, the demand for their services may very well rise which in turn could lead to more workers being hired at each and every possible wage rate. This would be in itself a valuable antirecession policy which could prove particularly important if, as is sometimes the case, it is not possible to reduce wage rates to any appreciable extent during recessions.

Increasing workers' productivity can take many forms from providing information about labor market conditions to retraining of workers and labor mobility assistance. For example, quite often workers are unaware that there are jobs available where their average productivity may be higher without their having to increase their level of skill; this is as important to management as it is to labor. Also, given this country's institutional framework, this may be the best time to help reshuffle labor toward expanding industries, for even during recessions some sectors of the economy may be expanding.

Forcing unemployed workers to work in any job as has been proposed, and is already being acted upon by some unemployment and welfare agencies (a topic to be discussed in some detail in the next section) or preventing firms from laying off unnecessary labor, as is sometimes the policy of unions, while there are industries needing labor, may simply serve to retard true recovery and/or slow down growth. This reshuffling of labor would not only assist some industries in proceeding with their expansion, but would also avoid their having to pay artificially created higher wage rates—for example, due to lack of information or inability of unemployed workers to move. This reshuffling may or may not necessitate some retooling of skills; if it does, it may serve to supplement other manpower policies aimed at the reshuffling of those workers. Finally, if and when retooling of the work force becomes an almost constant necessity, a period of recession may prove to be the best time to undertake this task. In this case, retooling would take, at least up to a certain point, the place of unemployment.

Manpower development is also important during the recovery and prosperity phases of the business cycle. Recovery may be considerably retarded if serious bottlenecks in production are allowed to develop due to the existence of labor shortages in specific skill groups. As was discussed earlier, in technologically advanced societies intersectoral transfers of labor may be difficult to accomplish within short periods of time. Manpower development can be effective in overcoming this sort of problem, for it is a way to cope with some of the market imperfections that can slow down the pace of recovery.[a] By reducing the chances of an abortive recovery, effective manpower development may discourage the government from using alternative policies which may prove to be, for example, inflationary in nature.

But manpower development is also capable of prolonging prosperity with a

---

[a]There is no inconsistency between this statement and the one made in Chapter 2. There the criticism was directed to specific forms of manpower development which are thought to be incompatible with the principles of market economics.

minimum of side effects like inflation. These two problems are closely related, but they are analytically different. The first could give rise initially to the co-existence of unemployment and inflation. The second could give rise to high employment and inflation; however, if inflation gets out of control this situation may degenerate into one of unemployment and inflation, too, whereas in the former, unemployment may or may not increase. In this connection, it might help to bear in mind the distorted pattern of investment that may result from inflation, and the adverse price expectations that it might create. Regardless of which one is worse or where the line between these two problems should be drawn, it seems clear that manpower development can assist in both instances. The closer the economy gets to full employment, the more important it is to match job vacancies and available workers in any effort to sustain prosperity under highly dynamic economic conditions. Failure to match them may result in the unemployment of others.

Concerning the so-called trade-off between inflation and unemployment, the available evidence seems to support the view that such a trade-off exists at any given one point in time; however, considerable disagreement exists with regard to its magnitude or final effect.[1] As Professor Milton Friedman has so forcefully explained, the monetary authorities cannot peg real magnitudes like the unemployment rate through their actions.[2] However, they can affect it, though the final direction seems today unclear once the dynamics of the process are considered. The fact that there is no simple way to predict how much unemployment is associated with different levels of price change does not mean such a relationship does not exist. This is not incompatible either with our previous statement whereby, above a certain point, increases in prices resulting from the inflationary process may cause unemployment to develop. This is simply a consequence of such a trade-off. At any rate, the important point is that increases in aggregate demand at the macro level can have more lasting and predictable effects on employment when manpower development policies can be implemented at the micro level so that a smoother process can be obtained.

In a recent paper, R. Meidner suggests how effective manpower development policies seem to have been in reducing the cost of the trade-off in inflation-prone economies.[3] In another paper, Professor M.S. Cohen estimates some of the manpower development policies used in the U.S. during the 1960s seem to have been partially successful in increasing employment beyond what might have been possible in the absence of such policies.[4] Limited as this evidence is, it does point to an increased realization of the central role that manpower development can play in this respect.

At this juncture, it is very important to stress that in a basically market-oriented economy manpower development policies are not supposed to prevent market disequilibrium and concomitant changes in relative prices. In principle, market disequilibrium is part and parcel of a market economy where consumers' decisions are supposed to determine, at least to a very large extent, the pattern of production. Manpower development policies are only intended to speed up and smooth out the process of adjustment towards a new market equilibrium.

Manpower development can also be most effective in steering the economy into a path of adequate rates of economic growth with a minimum of friction.[b] The faster the desired rate of economic growth, ceteris paribus, the greater the sacrifice a given society will have to make in order to obtain it. This is a very difficult challenge in a fundamentally democratic society, for the values and needs of the various participants have to be taken into account and they are bound to differ considerably. By way of illustration, any major attempt to improve the quality of environment within a short period of time may temporarily slow down the rate of gains in average productivity. While this is sought by many, for those who were hoping to gain from faster increases in productivity, it may be less appealing. The degree of sacrifice which economic growth imposes on a social group reflects largely the emergence of structural imbalances during the process of economic expansion.[c] In principle, these structural imbalances are similar to those that develop during the recovery and expansion phases of the business cycle. Faster desired rates of economic expansion simply tend to exacerbate them. This, in turn, makes the allocation function of the market mechanism a more difficult task.

A good example of some of the problems posed by this process is the apparent difficulty in absorbing rural migrants to the cities into the labor market, at least in the short run. It seems that due to differences in labor quality and in the expectations of the participants, considerable time is required to absorb them. As Professor Oscar Ornati recently indicated, we do not know with enough precision the way in which rural in-migrants are absorbed into the urban labor market, nor what are the adjustment problems they face.[5] Another example along the same lines is the apparent difficulty encountered in breaking in new young entrants into the labor force. In Chapter 1 it was noted that this group has been experiencing very high rates of unemployment for the last 15 or 20 years. Of course, our institutional framework has something to do with it; for example, minimum wage legislation, attitudes toward school dropouts, etc. However, blaming only these factors would be to take a very simplistic attitude toward the whole issue. These are examples where there is available labor which, with some help, could be transferred into productive employment, hence, facilitating a faster rate of economic expansion which does not involve a higher cost but rather a lower one, since many of these people are unemployed.

Helping to eliminate structural imbalances is thus one of the major tasks of manpower development. At any rate, it seems clear then that manpower development can be of great value in reducing the cost of the trade-off between the desired degree of economic expansion and the sacrifice which society has to make to attain it. Manpower development can speed up the restoration of equilibrium here, too, so that the process of economic growth can be smoother.

---

[b]At the level of generality at which the present analysis is being conducted, there seems no need to specify what is an adequate rate of economic growth, even if this could be done.

[c]Intersectoral imbalances tend to develop inflationary pressures. In addition, rapid economic growth requires more savings regardless of their source. It may also require that gains in productivity not be translated into fewer hours of work. The above examples illustrate what is meant by sacrifice.

In view of the very profound structural changes that are expected to occur during the coming years, some of which were discussed earlier in this study, this aspect of manpower development should be given considerable weight.

It is relevant to point out here that cyclical fluctuations and economic growth are not entirely unrelated processes. Rather, they tend to influence each other. This suggests that the trade-off that exists with regard to economic growth and the trade-offs that develop during the recovery and prosperity phases of the business cycle (and which were discussed earlier in this section) are not entirely independent of each other either, although they do represent different analytical phenomena and it is important to understand these differences in designing manpower development strategies. The fact is that they can reinforce each other, thus rendering the path of economic adjustment a more tortuous one to travel. This suggests that manpower development, by reducing the cost of both kinds of trade-off, can help to make the transition from sustained prosperity into economic growth an easier task. The cost in terms of lost production and employment, and human suffering in general, resulting from failure here are not only large but unrecoverable as our past experience has taught us.

Manpower development has as its central concern increasing labor productivity. This has turned out to be one of the major sources of economic growth in the United States.[6] Additions to capital stock and the labor supply alone could not have accounted for the outstanding performance of the American economy with regard to economic growth over the past 100 years. Increases in the average productivity of the factors of production were also necessary. This, of course, includes both better technology and higher labor quality. But it should be noted that the former depends considerably on improving the quality of labor, particularly high level manpower, for this makes possible the further development of knowledge which is at the heart of technological progress.

Continuously improving the quality of our human resource base is essential in any effort to maintain high rates of growth at the lowest possible cost. That rapid growth seems to require a continuous upgrading of the labor force is suggested by the persistence of high rates of return on practically all kinds and levels of training. As F. Welsh recently suggested, these high rates of return have persisted despite a significant increase in the output of qualified workers.[7] It would be difficult to account for this high rate of return if their training were not adding to production. All this suggests the very close association that seems to exist between manpower development and economic growth. This is of the greatest relevance for economic minorities, for making them more productive would contribute greatly to rapid economic growth. This would in itself represent a great contribution to any attempt to improve the quality of life in America.

The maximum technical capability of the economic system for growth and adjustment is an issue that has been of considerable interest to economists. One of the major tests to which the capability of the system for adjustment can be subject is that of conversion to and reconversion from war production. This usually encompasses occupational, industrial, and locational adjustments all together, and within a short span of time. (In this respect it differs from automation since this is influenced by the rate at which the system can absorb it, at least in a competitive economy). In this connection, the versatility of the American labor force has proved to be a very important asset. However, the more advanced the technology employed, and the more specific the job assignments, the more difficult this task is likely to become.

Long-run as well as short-run changes in labor force participation have played a central role in giving the American labor force a relatively high degree of flexibility. Manpower development can be of great value in conserving this huge reservoir of human resources so that the versatility of the American labor force can be maintained and, if possible, increased. For example, women may be willing to enter the labor force during this sort of transition period, but if they have been away from the labor force for a rather long time, their skills may have become obsolete. This conservation of the human resource base would help to insure that the technical capacity of the American economy for growth and adjustment be flexible rather than fixed.

It seems clear then that manpower development is an all-weather economic tool. This, among other reasons, suggests why it is important to have an ongoing manpower development strategy rather than a piece-meal one. Of course, the content of the manpower development package tends to vary from one situation to another according to the problem present, so that the manpower development package that can help reduce the cost of the trade-off between intersectoral imbalances and rapid economic growth is not necessarily the same as the manpower development package that would reduce the cost of the trade-off between unemployment and changes in the price level. And the manpower development package which may be justified in assisting unemployed workers during a recession may differ from that recommended to conserve human resources regardless of the level of economic activity. This does not mean, however, that a specific manpower development tool should not be included in more than one package. As discussed earlier, in most cases the various roles of manpower development are not entirely independent of one another. For example, extending the duration of economic prosperity contributes to the attainment of adequate levels of economic growth; retraining workers during recession can help match workers and job vacancies during the following expansion. Not only can specific manpower development tools be present in more than one package, but it is also important to realize that the various packages are not entirely independent of one another either.

A word of caution, however; a deliberate effort has been made to stress the important role of manpower development in giving flexibility to the system and in providing a greater chance for balanced growth. It is important, therefore, that manpower development policies do not themselves become petrified over the long run to the point of preventing the very change they are supposed to promote. This danger is always present when policies are implemented since they have to be carried out by a bureaucratic structure. This suggests that manpower development packages as well as specific tools should be subject to frequent review. Another point to be constantly borne in mind is that manpower development is a servant, not a master; that is, it should help the market mechanism to facilitate rather than hinder the adjustment to major changes in national objectives, such as the present shift toward increased preoccupation with improving the quality of the environment.

All this suggests how difficult it is to draw the line between manpower development strategies which try to improve the functioning of the market mechanism and those which try to dictate the direction of the market. The final decision must depend, as suggested earlier, on detailed empirical work as to the respective effect of various manpower development strategies upon the working of the labor market.

All in all, the most salient point in this analysis is the strategic role of manpower development. Effective manpower development can move the American economy closer to a situation where full employment, price stability and adequate rate of economic growth can all be achieved simultaneously. It seems to be the missing link in the struggle toward this goal. But, at the same time, it also contributes to the improvement of the quality of American life, not only by conserving the human resource base as a link between it and the labor market, but also by enhancing the capability of this country to tackle other nationally important problems related to the growth of the economy. All this can result in great benefits to economic minorities, which is the major concern of this study, since failure to solve any or all of these problems adversely affect economic minorities to a relatively greater extent than it does other groups in the United States.

The remainder of this section will focus on an analysis of manpower development amid various co-existing types of unemployment. This analysis will be very much in terms of the American experience during the post-war period, whereby each successive period of prosperity seems not only to have failed to eliminate unemployment, but has actually been accompanied by higher levels of unemployment, except for a short interlude during the second half of the 1960s when the average unemployment rate reached its lowest level since the Korean war. The significance of this was marred by the very special circumstances surrounding this period, namely the beginning of large scale involvement in Vietnam. It is therefore inconclusive regarding new trends. This issue has been at the center of the unemployment controversy among economists and has generally received widespread attention, particularly in view of the fact that the Employment Act of 1946 instructed the President of the United States to use all practical means at his disposal and to seek the cooperation of all major economic and political groups in promoting and maintaining maximum production and useful employment for all persons willing to work while preserving economic stability. He was instructed to do so, however, while fostering and promoting free enterprise. In principle then, the tenor of the Employment Act is quite consistent with the underlying philosophy of this study. Interestingly enough, no specific way as to how this command should be carried out was provided. One may wonder if this was a reflection of the lack of understanding of what was really involved in that policy, or of insufficient knowledge as to how such an endeavor could be accomplished at that time, though the idea that something along those lines was possible was gaining acceptance. With the passage of time, what started as a rather abstract command has become more concrete and comprehensible, as attested to by the development of fiscal, monetary, wage, manpower development and other policies. The recent sharp cut-backs in military expenditures at a time when the economy was beginning to slide amid rapid inflation, and the need to convert from war production, if only for the time being, are good reminders that the problem of high average levels of unemployment is still very prominent.

Table 3-1 shows the very significant effect of this change. Employment generated by defense expenditures hit a peak in 1968 (precisely at about the same time that unemployment reached a record low since the Korean conflict) and then declined sharply. Particularly significant is that most of the employment losses have occurred in the private sector of the economy and in military employment. The impact of this cut-back has been heavily concentrated not only industrially but occupationally and regionally as well. For example, semiskilled workers are a very important component of some of the most affected industries; geographically, California is likely to be one of the most affected states. The government has been fearful of using an aggressive fiscal policy because of the difficulties they have been experiencing in controlling inflation. This suggests the important role that manpower development could play in alleviating the adverse effect of this transition upon employment.

A significant challenge to manpower development is that in the designing of strategies to combat unemployment, account has to be taken of the fact that the various components of unemployment seem to be derived from different causes which might necessitate different cures. Before the President can be expected to apply the remedies of manpower development with some degree of success,

Table 3-1
Employment Attributable to Department of Defense Expenditures, for Selected Years

	(in thousands)		
	1965	1968	1971[a]
Total	5,759	8,129	6,354
Public employment	3,657	4,555	4,054
Federal military	2,716	3,460	3,034
Federal civilian	928	1,075	1,000
State and local	13	20	20
Private	2,102	3,574	2,300

[a]Estimate

Source: *Economic Report of the President*, 1971.

economists will have to conduct further testings of their theoretical explanations concerning the various causes of unemployment as well as of possible solutions. Also, they will have to improve their means of identifying the relative intensity of the various forms of unemployment during a given period of time. In this connection it should be pointed out, however, that some significant progress has already been made.

The two major forms of unemployment contending for the dubious honor of being the main type of unemployment plaguing the American economy throughout most of the post-war period were, and still are, demand unemployment and structural unemployment. The former was advanced by economists who saw levels of aggregate demand that were inadequate to provide full employment as the major cause of unemployment in the United States during this period. This group was formed mainly, but not exclusively, by macroeconomists, particularly of the Keynesian brand—economists who had studied the Great Depression and what could be accomplished in eliminating unemployment when aggregate demand is substantially increased, as it was during World War II and, to a lesser extent, during the Korean episode. These are economists influenced by the idea that the economic system may lack the self-correcting mechanism implied in Neoclassical economic thinking.[d] This influence seems to have permeated the drafting and passage of the Employment Act of 1946. Supporting this general view on unemployment was also the influential Council of Economic Advisors of the Kennedy era.

The structural unemployment school, on the other hand, comprised economists who saw as the major cause of unemployment during this period deep-rooted changes in the structure of the economy. These changes had resulted in pronounced intersectoral imbalances difficult to eliminate in the short-run because their elimination requires profound changes in the occupational, industrial and regional composition of the labor force. Most of the economists supporting this view were labor economists who were likely to be impressed by the very substantial changes that had taken place in the composition of the demand for labor and the pattern of industrial location, as well as by the extent of hidden unemployment, and who were also becoming increasingly aware of the possibility that the incidence of unemployment was concentrated by groups and regions.[e] It is interesting to observe that neither of these two groups made any deliberate effort to relate the problem to the possible existence of a wage structure that might have become out of line (given the need for adjustment). One might only speculate that they thought nothing could be done along this line.

While these two types of unemployment were at the heart of the unemployment controversy, it should be noted that they were not the only contenders.

[d]Keynes expounded the idea that unless corrective measures are undertaken, the economic system could be chronically in a condition of underemployment equilibrium rather than full employment equilibrium.

[e]The difference in training of the contending groups has been stressed because it helps explain the theoretical split.

Growth unemployment and frictional unemployment were also put forward as contributing to the problem. Growth unemployment can be viewed as a hybrid of the two major types of unemployment discussed before. On the one hand, a very large influx of inexperienced and often ill-equipped workers were starting to enter the labor force. On the other hand each successive period of recovery was not being accompanied by a strong underlying rate of economic growth, given the potential for growth of the economy; therefore, the recovery was failing to absorb all of the new entrants into the labor force. This explains the use of the term growth unemployment. Higher levels of aggregate demand could have provided the means to employ more workers, but if they were ill-equipped to fill the newly created jobs they would remain unemployed, slowing down the process of economic expansion. This explains the hybrid character of this form of unemployment.

Frictional unemployment, on the other hand, is said to be present when vacancies exist and there are qualified workers who could fill them but, due to frictions (imperfections) in the system, some time is needed before they can fill the vacant jobs.[8] It is usually measured as a residual. If the time it takes to match unemployed job seekers and vacancies increases, this form of unemployment tends to become a type of structural unemployment;[f] for example, the longer a worker stays out of work the greater the chance that his skill may have deteriorated. The argument was that frictional unemployment was rising quite independently of purely structural causes. This was blamed on the increased seriousness of some labor market imperfections, particularly lack of adequate information under rapidly changing labor market conditions.

It is interesting to notice how the unemployment issue goes far beyond the recession situation and cuts across various levels of economic activity. This suggests why it has to be examined within the broader context of manpower development in general.

Accompanying this controversy on unemployment was another reality: the market mechanism was becoming, in general, relatively more imperfect. Economic concentration was intensifying. Unions were increasing their power in the already unionized sectors of the economy, and there is some evidence that the effect of this power was being transmitted to other sectors of the economy as well—witness the trend in automatic wage increases as part of collective agreement. It is precisely this combination of concentration in business and union power that seems to have been most effective in affecting the wage outcome and, therefore, unemployment. Moreover, the National Labor Relations Board, in its attempt to buy industrial peace, has been creating new obstacles for the efficient functioning of the market mechanism—witness the trend in long-term labor contracts and in centralized collective bargaining which

---

[f]Indeed, sometimes these two types of unemployment are not distinguished clearly. It should be noted, however, that in the frictional case, there are workers who have the necessary qualifications to fill the vacancies. On the other hand, in the structural case, workers lack these qualifications, at least within the same labor market.

tend to give rise to wage decisions where relatively little consideration is given to short-run market conditions and differences in labor market needs.

The unemployment issue was not merely an academic exercise, but a very real challenge for policymakers. The standard argument was that if inadequate levels of aggregate demand were at fault then fiscal and monetary policies could at least be tried. On the other hand, if structural unemployment were the villain, this set of remedies would be of no help; it would only lead the economy into the abyss of inflation and eventually even more unemployment, as was discussed earlier. For structural unemployment, the standard remedy would have to be sought in an active manpower development policy. As for the other two contenders, since growth unemployment was thought to be a hybrid of the other two types and frictional unemployment was largely seen as a special case of the structural variety, the above policy recommendations could be extended to them at least in terms of broad strategy.

Note the absence of any reference to encouraging a more plastic external wage structure—that is a wage structure more responsive to change. In a sense, this represents a defeatist attitude toward the system of free markets, a Galbraithian attitude. It is also significant that there seems to have been little realization of the possible interaction between structural unemployment and demand unemployment. Changes in aggregate demand intended to cure the latter may generate structural unemployment if they call for a change in the composition of aggregate demand that affects the relative importance of the various skills used in its production. Structural unemployment, on the other hand, can, in turn, cause a decrease in aggregate demand, therefore generating demand unemployment or the hybrid growth type of unemployment.[9]

It is worth noting that both sides in the controversy were able to amass a considerable amount of evidence in support of their respective positions. This is less surprising, however, when it is recognized that the apparent confusion was due largely to the coexistence of both sets of forces, or to be more precise, to the coexistence of all four types of unemployment. This suggests that what was required was to mount an attack on all fronts—a fact finally understood, if only partially, on the part of policymakers.[g] On the one hand efforts were made to stimulate demand, with the growing realization that the stimulus would have to be sufficiently strong to absorb a rapidly expanding labor force. Budget deficits, tax credits, tax revisions and foreign trade expansion were all tried in different degrees as major forms of employment policy.[h] On the other hand, active manpower development policies were also instituted. It is these policies that will be examined at a later stage in this study.

Launching an attack against unemployment on all fronts seems to have been a step in the right direction; however, due to the central role of manpower

[g]It is beyond the scope of this study to inquire into the success of any specific line of attack. The main concern here is with the fact that there was a need to cure all types of unemployment that were causing the problem, and that this was partially appreciated.

[h]In a situation like this, the line between economic recovery and economic growth becomes somewhat blurred.

development in making the major goals of the American economy more nearly compatible with one another, some degree of coordination would have been desirable. Professor Richard A. Lester has pointed to the dualism that exists at the highest level of decision-making, namely Congress and the Executive Branch.[10] At this level the demand side (employment policy) and the supply side (manpower development policy) are not coordinated at all, which tends to reduce their effectiveness in combating unemployment. However, this should not preclude acknowledgment of the progress that has already been made. At least it is much better understood today than ever before that increases in aggregate demand are not in themselves sufficient to cause unemployment to disappear (as a matter of fact they could aggravate it temporarily, due to the interaction of the various forms of unemployment), and that the training of people for non-existent jobs may be to no avail and merely a source of further frustration. Besides, it is important to realize that the line between too much coordination and outright planning of the economy is not an absolute one and better communication among the various groups responsible for these policies may be the most one should expect, or even desire. This approach is ingrained in the American political process of checks and balances; for example, an analogous situation exists concerning the power of Congress to spend and to tax, or even between the design and control of monetary and fiscal policies.

It is interesting to note the slow but gradual transformation that seems to have occurred in the interpretation of what was involved in the 1946 Employment Act. At first not too much attention was given to manpower development. Gradually, however, an increased realization developed that the concept is central to any effort to encourage and promote prosperity with stability, under rapidly changing economic conditions. This illustrates clearly the plasticity of American institutions for the most part and why sometimes it is better, in dealing with such complex issues, to give general directives than to establish rigid formulae, no matter how efficient they might appear from a short-run point of view.

It is very difficult, to say the least, to estimate the relative importance of the various forms of unemployment. For one thing, their relative importance tends to change over time. Nevertheless, it is important to have at least some idea of their magnitude. From a practical point of view, the most important to estimate is structural-frictional unemployment because demand-growth unemployment tends to vary with the level of economic activity much more than the former.[i] Given the economic conditions of the 1950s and 1960s, structural unemployment has been estimated to be somewhere between 2 percent and 3 percent of the labor force;[11] major transformations in the composition of demand or the structure of production have affected them over time. In addition, frictional unemployment has been placed at between 1.5 percent and 2.5 percent of the labor force. It is this author's impression, however, that in computing these

---

[i]That structural and frictional unemployment are also affected by fluctuations in economic activity is obvious from the interaction among the major forms of unemployment discussed before.

estimates, proper account has not been taken of unemployment among the working poor. Of course, this aspect of unemployment is more hybrid in nature than is purely structural unemployment. Also, changes in labor force participation tend to cloud the meaning of any estimate in this area. For example, there seems to be some evidence that some long-term unemployed workers eventually drop out of the labor force. A similar situation may exist regarding the never placed, that is those who have never had a job and who are therefore difficult to account for. Finally, the very significant increase in subsidized education and the increase in the draft may have caused some underestimation of this form of unemployment. The above figures, when put together, serve only as a rough estimate of the minimum rate of unemployment that would exist if no demand-growth unemployment were present, that is between 3.5 percent and 5.5 percent of the labor force at a minimum.j

In the absence of specific efforts to reduce these two forms of unemployment, these figures could be used as a rough indication of how far employment could be expanded without any serious threat of inflation and major distortions in the pattern of resource allocation. The fact that there is some evidence that the manpower development programs of the 1960s helped to reduce the rate of unemployment during this period is a very encouraging sign, for this was done with only experimental, piecemeal efforts and with inadequate coordination with other economic policies, not to mention very limited funds. It is also important to bear in mind that profound disagreement exists as to how effective these other policies have been (for example monetary and fiscal) and even as to whether they may have been misused. These reservations must be borne in mind when considering the figures quoted above.

From unemployment as a recession problem, one must travel a considerable distance to come to grips with unemployment as a multidimensional phenomenon, thus creating a bridge between unemployment and povery, growth, etc.—particularly poverty as a group phenomenon due in large measure to institutional factors and not to the failure of the free market system. What is surprising is not that unemployment exists, but that it has not been higher due to the numerous restrictions that have been imposed—with the blessing at times of the government—on the free operation of the market. This suggests more than anything else what a very powerful mechanism the market is, for even working with handicaps it has been able to do a reasonably good job. Because the wage structure has not been allowed to adjust freely to changing market conditions, it is that we have been suggesting the use of manpower development to help ease the problems of adjustment.

---

jExtreme care has to be exercised in using estimates like the one above. Some knowledge would have to be available concerning the distribution of unemployment in different labor markets. Also, how responsive labor force participation is to change in level of economic activity.

4 Manpower Development and Economic Security

This section will be devoted to an analysis of manpower development within the broader context of economic security. Primarily, it should be noted that manpower development is in itself a form of economic security; for in a market-oriented economy, the main form of economic security is people's ability to earn an income from work, and manpower development has as its major goal to help people participate in the production process in an effective way by keeping their productive capacity at the highest possible level without interruption.

The provision of economic security is one of the greatest challenges confronting industrial societies, especially those subject to rapid technological change. A market economy might continue to be viable only if satisfactory means are found to cope with the problems posed by lack of adequate levels of economic security. This is an issue of the utmost importance in a study in which the underlying philosophy is the preservation of the market system. However, to discuss the role of the market mechanism without reference to the kind of society involved as well as its level of development would be of little value. The difference between what is required to make an industrial society workable and what is required to enable the market mechanism to distribute economic resources, and therefore income, efficiently, is a misunderstood subject. The market mechanism, if allowed to work, is neutral regarding who gets what; that is, it is impersonal. If and when a person cannot participate in the production process it leaves him out—he is unable to earn an income. However, he is still forced to enter the market as a consumer. The market mechanism dictates a certain income distribution that may or may not be acceptable to a given industrial society. (If it is not, society can alter it without having to renounce the market mechanism.) This suggests that means have to be developed to allow those who are left out to enter the market as consumers if the system is to be viable and/or to distribute income in a different way than the market would if left to itself, if this is considered desirable. That is, whether people are employed or not, they are an overhead cost to society since somehow they have to find a way to support themselves and their families.

Industrialization is almost always associated with urbanization and with the breakdown of traditional forms of family structure. It is under these conditions that economic security becomes a vital issue, for the average individual has nowhere to turn when he is unable to earn an income, unless a system exists to assist him. As long as a realistic minimum amount of economic security consistent with accepted social values exists, there is no reason why the market should not be able to perform well unless it is artificially impeded. It is only when this minimum amount of economic security is not available that workers and other groups try to strangle the market mechanism in order to protect their own position. Thus without a minimum of economic security, change is likely to be painful if only temporarily. Yet, change is essential for progress.

A person does not have to be an advocate of socialism to believe that without this minimum of economic security, modern industrial life is almost unbearable. This is true regardless of the political system or the mechanism used to allocate economic resources, and a capitalistic, market-oriented economy is no exception. It is regrettable that most of the attacks launched against this lack of economic security have been wrongly directed at the market mechanism as a resource allocator. It is likely that this is in part a result of the fact that many a person who claims a belief in the system of free enterprise and in conservatism towards change has never practiced his belief. Also, that politically myopic leaders have oftentimes failed to impress this point on their constituents. It is worth noting that the market mechanism is capable of allocating economic security, too (since this is a purchasable item), except for those who have been unable to enter the production process at any time. Even in the case where the income distribution dictated by the working of a free market is unacceptable to society and other forms of income distribution have to be sought, the market can still be effective except that it has to work within this constraint. At the risk of overemphasizing this point, it is important to remember that the market mechanism has proved capable of adjusting to different sets of constraints, such as a socially dictated minimum level of education, or child labor legislation.

Once the need to provide economic security in an industrial society is widely recognized and accepted, then, following the underlying philosophy of this study, it becomes necessary to find such means of providing economic security as will not interfere with the efficient functioning of the market system in allocating scarce economic resources, and which will also be socially and politically viable.

Before proceeding, there is a point which needs stressing: manpower development strategies and economic security strategies should be conceived together for maximum effect, due to their close interrelation. For example, by helping people to stay in or return to the labor market, society is helping to prevent the onset of economic insecurity. It will become apparent from this study that manpower development policies may very well fail to work unless they are adequately supplemented with other forms of economic security. It should be noted that the whole issue of economic security is of the utmost importance for economic minorities. It is precisely economic insecurity, and the inadequate means to cope with it, that tend to make them economic minorities.

That economic insecurity exists in the United States is not an issue which can be seriously contended. Whatever disagreement might exist centers on the question of degree. Officially classified as poor were close to 25 million people in the United States in 1969, even though the economy was operating at very high levels. This represents approximately 13 percent of this nation's population.[1] Some 5 to 6 million of the people who were working during the 1960s failed to earn more than $2,500 per year from their work and yet were not generally eligible for assistance. The above does not include people who at one time or another found themselves temporarily out of work for different reasons and who faced economic insecurity even though they were not officially classified as poor. This does not necessarily mean that the people of this country have failed to recognize the problem ensuing from economic insecurity in an industrial society, for there are few who have not at one time or another experienced the threat or anguish of economic insecurity. Rather, it means that no sooner have they started to cope effectively with some of the nation's existing problems than new ones have made their appearance, or the old problems have become more complex.

A look at the evolution of the means to cope with economic insecurity in the United States attests to the fact that the people of this country are quite aware of the economic insecurity issue. Only some 40 years ago this country entirely lacked a Social Security system. Now the possibility of some form of guaranteed minimum income is no longer a mere abstraction. However, in a basically democratic political system where many different values—sometimes conflicting—have to be taken into account the process of adjusting to new situations tends to be slow. Also, more and more people in this country have found ways to cope with economic insecurity independently. This is, in part, a reflection of the general level of affluence but also of a deliberate effort on the part of some of those people to control the forces of the market for their own advantage. Not everyone has access to these means of ensuring economic security, however, particularly if their financial means are limited. This raises a serious problem for those who have succeeded, even if only partially; do not feel the same need to continue the search for new methods to reduce economic insecurity and if they happen to have a strong political base they can exercise considerable influence in this respect.[a]

At this point, it seems appropriate to discuss the underlying philosophy of the American Social Security system, for it has been the central mechanism in this nation's battle to protect its people against economic insecurity. This will also assist in deciding whether and to what extent this system is worth saving in any effort to integrate manpower development and economic security strategies. First, the Social Security system attempts to provide only a first line of defense against economic insecurity. It is feared that if more than just a bare minimum were provided, people would, in general, lack the incentive to look after their own needs as far as possible. Whether this be true or not is, of course, an empirical matter, but one of the greatest importance. Second, it relies heavily on the insurance approach. However, as applied in the United States there is some difference between private insurance and social insurance. In the former case,

---

[a]One of the best illustrations one can hope to offer is the case of many American workers who have moved into the middle economic stratum. They have been protecting themselves, if only partially, by either obtaining fringe benefits or buying assets or both.

people receive benefits commensurate with what they have contributed; in the latter, people receive benefits that reflect their contributions, but the concept of social adequacy also enters into it in general.

The above two principles on which the American Social Security system seems to have been built are not in basic conflict with the main tenets of market economics. This should not be construed as a blanket endorsement of the way the system has functioned thus far. But a distinction must be made between whether it is the functioning of the system that might be defective or the underlying philosophy that is unacceptable.

There are three major criticisms that have been raised, not so much against the principles outlined above, as against the way the system has tended to work in the past. First, it does not protect everyone who potentially could be covered or provide against all causes of economic insecurity. Particularly the former problem has been a critical one, for groups have been added slowly and there is usually some lapse of time before people become entitled to benefits. For example, only about 84 percent of those currently 65 years old and over are receiving Old Age Survivor and Disability Insurance (OASDI) benefits and only some 90 percent of all paid employees are eligible for such benefits in the future. Second, what is considered a "first line of defense" has not been subject to frequent revision so that the system could keep pace with the higher standards of prosperity enjoyed by this country. This lag in adjustment has always been a serious matter. For example, for most types of economic insecurity, the International Labor Organization has been inclined to recommend that, on the average, a minimum of approximately 50 percent of the regular income from work should be covered. Originally among those covered by the various programs, this might have been so but by now, in many of the programs, the recipient gets considerably less than he would earn if employed. For instance, in the case of workers other than unskilled labor, it is doubtful if unemployment insurance covers more than one third.

Workers in the U.S. have tried to fill in these gaps in the American Social Security system by resorting to fringe benefits to be extracted at the bargaining table; fringe benefits over and above those required by law have become a larger share of labor costs, approximately 30 percent by now.[b] Even if it is taken into account that some fringe benefits are not entirely directed to meeting the challenge of economic insecurity, there is still, on the average, nearly one fourth of the total payroll left which is so directed. During the early stages of the big union era of 1935 to 1950, unions fought for higher wages and union security as their most important targets. But once they had consolidated their position, they shifted their emphasis toward greater economic security for their members. This trend has been recently accentuated by the challenge of automation. It is sometimes argued that fringe benefits have been obtained in lieu of higher wages,

---

[b]In a sample of 79 identical companies prepared by the Chamber of Commerce, it was found that fringe payments had increased from approximately 16 percent of payroll in 1947 to nearly 30 percent by 1967.[2]

and there seems to be some element of truth in this argument. In the experience of this author, however, less competitive industries seem to be paying relatively more in the form of fringe benefits than more competitive industries. This suggests, at least to some extent, it is monopoly power which allows them to pay relatively higher fringe benefits and, therefore, they are not always obtained in lieu of higher wages.[3] Even if workers were engaging in this form of trade-off, the fact still remains it is usually accompanied by reduced worker mobility, since staying with the employer is usually a prerequisite to cash in on these fringe benefits.

All this raises a major philosophical issue concerning the extent to which American industry should be expected to underwrite economic security in the United States. To be consistent with the major philosophy of this study, American industry ought to protect workers against economic insecurity only to the extent that there are risks involved in the actual production of the goods, and in this case, consumers should be expected to carry the burden of the cost of producing the goods. They should not, however, be expected to protect workers against economic insecurity in general, for this should be done through the Social Security system, at least insofar as minimum protection is concerned. The more firms with a high degree of monopoly power are able to subsidize the economic security of their workers, the greater the risk that the American economy may generate dualism, whereby some workers are and some workers are not adequately protected—a very thorny political issue.

The third major criticism usually raised against the present system is that the insurance principle is not suitable in the case of those who cannot be rehabilitated and who have not been previously covered by the insurance machinery of the system. The criticism here seems to be fundamentally against the inadequate provisions that have been made in this country to aid this group of people, particularly that it is not seen as a matter of right.

The public assistance feature of the system has virtually broken down. For example very few states have provisions to aid, through public assistance, families with dependent children in which the father is unemployed. Yet, not only is the coverage of unemployment inadequate in most cases, but some workers are not even covered, or not covered beyond a certain number of weeks (usually 26), which may prove grossly inadequate where structural unemployment is involved. Recently, some attempts have been made to remedy some of these problems; however, this feature of the system still leaves a lot to be desired, particularly the Poor Laws influence that seems to permeate the system.[4] Some state and local governments have been reluctant to accept the Public Assistance program and many have not even made use of all its potential, even though over 50 percent of the program is currently paid from federal funds.

Besides the above three major criticisms, it should also be noted that the American Social Security program is administered largely by local and state governments rather than being centralized at the federal level. This is quite consistent with the political organization of this country. However, most of the criticism against the present system is really the result of this administrative structure and the many inequalities in which it has resulted, due to the very considerable inter-state variations in the administration of the program. For example, some states provide for up to 39 weeks of covered unemployment while the vast majority have stuck to something close to 26 weeks. The level of payment under the various subprograms also tends to differ considerably; however, where this issue is most critical is with respect to the Public Assistance program. Furthermore, the number of programs vary somewhat from state to state; so do eligibility requirements which tend to reduce interregional mobility. Indeed, considerable disagreement exists as to what can be done about all of these problems besetting the American Social Security system.

Despite all its shortcomings, the policy of making transfer payments of various kinds has decidedly alleviated the incidence of economic insecurity in the United States and in so doing has helped to make our industrial society a viable proposition, at least for the time being (transfer payments refer to payments by the government for which it does not receive goods or services in return). But most important, it has laid down the foundations for the development of better programs and strategies. In a nutshell, it has shown the American people that economic insecurity can be conquered to a large extent without having to abandon the basic principles on which this society has grown.

Recently, the Tax Foundation reported that about 26 million people were receiving Social Security payments and another 14 million people were receiving public assistance.[5] This is approximately one fifth of the population of the United States; it suggests the significant progress that has been made in the battle against economic insecurity. (This does not include private efforts which are even more substantial.) However, the battle is far from over and new twists may be in the offing as our economy keeps on changing. It is with the alleviation of poverty that this study is particularly concerned.

Professor C. Green has estimated, for example, that in 1961 transfer payments rescued approximately 11.3 million people (or approximately 5 million families) from poverty.[6] Transfer payments, however, did not provide adequate protection for some 27.2 million people (or approximately 9 million families) in that same year. His definition of poverty level is fairly consistent with that used, in general, by U.S. government agencies, that is, those below this level represent clear cut cases of absolute poverty. Another estimate suggests that approximately 40 percent of social security benefits accrue to households which would be poor but for these benefits.[7] The table below suggests the extent to which poverty seems to be alleviated by the major forms of transfer payments and the extent to which they appear to have closed the pre-transfer poverty gap.

All these estimates strongly support the view that transfer payments of one kind or another have made a significant contribution to the war against poverty in the United States, but that they are still quite inadequate to eliminate it. Their major shortcoming may have been the limited assistance made available to the poorest group among those in the lowest income brackets—for the most part those who have been able to contribute little to the production process—and the

Table 4-1
Percentage of Total Transfer Payments that were Made to the Poor in 1966, by Major Type of Program

	Percentage of Households Receiving Transfers which were Poor before Transfer	Percentage of Transfers which Reduced the Pre-transfer Poverty Gap
Total transfer	49%	37%
OASDI	55	40
Unemployment Insurance	12	12
Workmen's Compensation	11	13
Veterans Pensions	50	39
Veterans Compensation	9	7
Public Assistance	77	77

Source: Irene Lurie, *The Distribution of Transfer Payments among Households*, in the President's Commission on Income Maintenance Programs, 1970.

lack of aid to the working poor who, under the present system, are ineligible for public assistance regardless of family income and need.

In closing, it ought to be observed that some of these programs do not represent necessarily net income redistribution, but only forms of purchasing economic security as a group. Net income redistribution may occur because of the compulsory character of social insurance in the United States and because benefits do not always correspond directly to contributions. This reflects the fact that in building this nation's Social Security system, the concept of social adequacy was included which makes it differ, to some extent, from the principle involved in private insurance. Only in the case of public assistance does a redistribution of income take place, for recipients of public assistance are, for the most part, unable to contribute to their own protection. This then is quite in line with market principles whereby anybody who can afford to purchase his own protection should do so.

In discussing economic insecurity with reference to manpower development policies, four major groups of people should be distinguished. The first group is comprised of people who are potential employable workers from a social, as well as an economic, point of view. If and when adequately equipped to enter the labor market, they can earn an income which is considered socially adequate for their own support and that of their families. This is, of course, assuming that a realistic social minimum income is considered and which most people would agree should not be less than the minimum wage in existence at any point in time ($3,800 to $4,200 currently). Until their labor market rehabilitation is completed, with the aid of manpower development programs, ways would have to be designed to provide this group with a socially acceptable minimum income.

The second group is formed by people who are economically employable but not socially.[c] They could be equipped to earn an income from work but not one which would be considered socially adequate. (Here it is possible to include those in group one who may find their income from work inadequate due to family size.) In this case, manpower development policies would have to be accompanied by what is tantamount to permanent income supplements, otherwise these people would become the working poor, that is those whose income from work is socially inadequate. They do not differ in principle from the working poor of today, except that many of them could be subject to manpower rehabilitation. The alternative would be to support them totally. This is a very complex issue that raises a major philosophical issue, for income supplements could be viewed, in this case, as a kind of permanent subsidy for the producers employing this category of workers. This may be considered undesirable or not in line with what society's own conception of what a social minimum really entails, particularly in view of the many uncertainties that exist concerning the impact of future technological development upon the skill composition of the demand for labor.[d]

In the third group are people who have lost—temporarily or permanently—their earning capacity. For this group, income maintenance programs are required. Those whose earning capacity is partially impaired need only income supplements similar to those recommended for the second group. Manpower development programs should be used here to the extent that they can help in rehabilitation. It is possible to include here the special case of those who, due to age, find their average productivity declining. The present institutional framework sometimes prevents adjustments that would keep these people employed at reduced rates—frequently, at still relatively high rates due to their experience, etc. The available evidence, limited as it is, suggests that many operations can be simplified and/or modified or the worker can be transferred in order to meet this problem, and that management is frequently quite willing (if allowed) to undertake such changes. The institutional framework in which these decisions are made should be made more flexible than it now is.

Finally, there are those people who cannot be rehabilitated through manpower development programs to enable them to earn an income from work. For this group, an adequate guaranteed minimum income seems to be the only alternative to economic insecurity.

This analysis is cast in rather abstract terms, assuming that resources could be made available. If on the other hand, resources were very limited, as they appear to be today, it is possible that most of those who need manpower development assistance might never become highly productive and, therefore, if expected to work, might need permanent income supplements. This is relevant in the current polemic on this subject, for there appear to be people who think social and

---

[c]The term economically employable is being used here in a rather loose sense because anybody who can add to production is economically employable if willing (and allowed) to work for the value of his marginal revenue product.

[d]Account would have to be taken of the effect that any decision in this area may have upon the international trade position and the international trade relations of this country.

economic rehabilitation is a short-term process. Society will have to decide how many of these people it really wants to rehabilitate and how fast to do it. This is very important in the case of economic minorities, as will be discussed in the next chapter.

Protection against economic insecurity is being discussed currently in academic and political circles in terms of two alternatives. They are the guaranteed minimum income and the guaranteed job, though the former has been particularly discussed in many different forms. Each has different, but quite definite, implications for manpower development which should not be ignored. Somehow there has been a tendency to discuss them as if they were only indirectly connected with manpower development. Fortunately this attitude seems to be changing. The significance of the issue can be seen in that economists holding all kinds of philosophical views, as well as scholars in related disciplines, have thrown their hats into the ring and have debated the issue.

The guaranteed income strategy is usually cast in terms of a socially defined minimum income based on family size, with no strings attached and no means test. It is viewed primarily as a substitute for the present system of public assistance. Some of its advocates have recognized, however, the need to retain some of the services provided currently by welfare agencies due to the particular needs of some welfare clients, such as the mentally and physically handicapped, orphans, etc. Some advocates of this approach have gone as far as to recommend that this program replace completely the present social security machinery, or have talked about a national dividend whereby every person is guaranteed a share of the income of the nation which would be his minimum income. Any income from work would be above and beyond this national dividend. Most advocates of the guaranteed minimum income have seen the possible effect that this approach may have upon work incentive and, therefore, on the supply of effort, regardless of the particular mechanism used; hence, several schemes to provide work incentive have been suggested.

In general, it seems desirable, at the very least, to ensure that those with higher earnings, before any such program is instituted, will still be assured of higher incomes after it is implemented. This, of course, does not mean that the relative gap between different income groups would not be altered, only that their relative position would not change, otherwise considerable dislocations in the supply of effort may result. In devising such a system it is important to take into account not only the effect of the program on those receiving the benefits, but also the effect on those who may have to pay taxes to support the program. This is a problem which apparently has not received adequate attention.[8]

Society would have to decide how important it is to encourage work, and thus whether to relate the schedule of payments and the extent to which they are taxed, to work effort or not. Professor H.J. Aaron, for one, has proposed a very interesting idea which is presented here only to illustrate the difficulties involved.[9] He has suggested that incomes be taxed at rates reflecting the ability of the recipient to work. Those who are unable to work would be taxed at relatively high rates whereas those who are able to work would be taxed at relatively low rates. However, these lower tax rates would be accompanied by smaller basic grants and vice versa. This suggests that payments to the working poor would be graduated positively with respect to hours of work and negatively to hourly wage rates. This means that if a worker's wage rate rises, his bonus would decline, but his total income would increase. This and other similar proposals reflect the underlying fear that, in principle, the guaranteed minimum income mechanism could adversely affect the willingness to work of many of those involved in the program.

The practical question seems to hinge partially on what kind of tax rates to use, that is whether the marginal rates should decrease or not. It is important to bear in mind that effects of taxes, as well as of changes in income on work, are subject to two factors: the substitution effect and the income effect, which tend to work in opposite directions. On one hand, the opportunity cost of leisure is affected but, on the other hand, the ability to purchase leisure is also affected. At present, little is known about the possible net effect of these two forces on the various groups involved. For example, it is possible that high quality labor may be encouraged to increase (decrease) their aggregate effort, whereas low quality labor may be encouraged to decrease (increase) theirs. Also, as the relative position of people in society is changed so are their values, which include those toward work. Furthermore, the work behavior of other members of the family has to be considered, too, and there are many unknowns here.

One major problem is that no concensus exists concerning the kind of coordination that should be created between this sort of scheme and the present tax system. Opinions range from complete separation to total integration. Those who are more concerned with the political realities of this attempt seem to be inclined to a dual structure, but with some coordination to avoid basic conflicts between the two structures, particularly for borderline situations. In this regard, whatever the final choice, one important consideration is that incomes below the break-even income—namely that above which no benefits are received—should not be subject to regular personal income taxation, because in this event, it is possible for a family to be subject to both the offsetting tax on the basic allowance (which is part of most schemes) and the regular personal income tax. Table A-15 shows an example of this dual taxation.

All this suggests that finding viable solutions to the work incentive problem deserves further exploration, particularly if the guaranteed income philosophy were to emerge victorious from the present ideological dispute. At the present stage of development, however, the effect of a guaranteed income and of any such incentive scheme on the labor force is uncertain.[10] One thing is clear, whatever the effect, it will have some serious impact on manpower development, which is why this kind of information is so important in the development of a combined strategy.

In principle, guaranteed minimum income schemes can be coordinated with manpower development policies designed to rehabilitate—socially and economically—those recipients of such an income who could effectively benefit from these policies. The whole is potentially greater than the sum of the parts;

coordination would render these two sets of policies more effective than they are likely to be separately.

The guaranteed income solution to the problem of economic insecurity appears very attractive, at least in general terms, to many who would like to optimize, as far as possible, the efficiency of the market mechanism. It would tend to remove the truly unemployables from the market place without making them a prey to economic insecurity, for they could still enter the market as consumers. Unemployment figures would then reflect, more accurately, the real unemployment existing in the economy during any specific period of time. This would greatly facilitate the implementation of other major economic policies if this is desired. Moreover, if permitted, the market mechanism would then be more nearly free to improve its performance in allocating resources which should result in a greater output of goods and services. This would, in turn, render the task of transferring resources to support people unable to work relatively easier.

All of this is viable only if the productive groups are willing to transfer sufficient resources—as socially defined—for the adequate support of the economically unproductive. This transfer of resources would have to include the support of manpower development programs, too, if this is deemed socially desirable. This author remains unconvinced of the willingness of the productive group to transfer sufficient resources to carry out such a task at reasonable levels, while the unproductive group is politically too weak to insure such a result—though they are currently increasing their relative position, politically speaking, through the very existence of manpower and other related agencies which are serving incipiently as a power base. Moreover, this author has not been persuaded that a sufficiently large number of market imperfections would be removed so that the market mechanism could operate closer to its optimum. One of the major obstacles seems to be that the major source of tax revenue is the income of the American middle income group. This group appears to be convinced not only that it is overburdened with taxes, but also that the present tax structure is grossly inequitable. Until this can be remedied there would be strong opposition to any such level of resource transfer as might be required for this strategy to be effective. However, revision of the tax system is part and parcel of the whole problem and this ought to be made clear.

Although the manpower development program would add to the short-term cost of such a program, it could greatly reduce the long-term costs by returning as many people as can benefit from it back to production, thus adding to income and reducing transfer payments.

This approach to economic insecurity has also been of interest to those who want to insure that everyone shares in the growing prosperity of this nation in an almost automatic fashion, by assuring everyone of a minimum participation through some form of social dividend. This would mean that everyone could participate in the growth of the economy if only from the consumption side. They are not concerned about the effect of this plan on work participation, for they consider such minimum participation a matter of right. Although the idea is compatible with manpower development programs, it has usually been discussed as a separate objective to be undertaken regardless of the final philosophy adopted with respect to the latter. It is intriguing to observe how the same idea has been so appealing to two groups whose views are in other respects so divergent.

The implementation of this approach to economic security presents a major sociological challenge. The economically unproductive group would have to find alternative ways of investing its time. There is no place for subsidized employment in this scheme in its purest form, at least not in principle, although it could be incorporated by retaining the category of socially working poor. At present there is widespread skepticism regarding the capacity of this society to cope with such a challenge, particularly if the ranks of the economically unproductive are swollen—for example, as a result of a quickening of the pace of technological progress without adequate employment substitutes. This problem should not be too serious, however, if limited only to people beyond market rehabilitation. The question of who would be included in this group depends largely on society's commitment to massive, long-range market rehabilitation manpower development schemes. If it is very much committed to this goal then the possibility of this group ever becoming large would be greatly reduced. Unfortunately, at this time this is a highly speculative subject.

The second major approach to the solution of economic insecurity which is currently in vogue in the United States involves the guarantee of a job. It could be viewed as an extreme interpretation of the 1946 Employment Act. The guaranteed job approach implies a particular manpower development strategy. This does not mean it cannot be coordinated with other forms of manpower development, but the latter would have to be viewed as secondary to the more general manpower development strategy underlying this philosophy. In this respect, it differs from the guaranteed minimum income mechanism for the latter can be coordinated more freely with various manpower development strategies.

The manpower development strategy implied in the guaranteed job scheme may give rise to a paradoxical situation. If a person is obliged, at least on paper, to spend his whole day working, one may wonder what time he will have to devote to his labor market rehabilitation—particularly where this rehabilitation is long-term in nature—which, if he is expected eventually to stand by himself in the labor market, is essential. It is obvious that this is of more than just passing interest for economic minorities, for the objective of this group is to be able to stand independently in the labor market.

The guaranteed job strategy is generally conceived in terms whereby the government stands as an employer of last resort. The strategy's advocates expect to reduce the cost of providing the people involved with an income because they would, by virtue of the plan, be adding to production. This is not necessarily the case, however. It seems that underlying this method of coping with economic insecurity is the belief that the vast majority receiving public assistance in the United States are capable of productive work—a view that has predominated for years in public assistance programs. Yet, it is a theory which has not so far been empirically validated. It is a fact that current levels of public assistance are grossly inadequate; for example, general assistance programs, on the average, pay $45 to $55 per month in the United States. But the range is very wide, varying from approximately $10 in low average payment states and $110 in high average payment states.

The same story applies to other public assistance programs. With very few exceptions these payments are generally insufficient to cover even what is considered the minimum standard cost for basic needs. It is difficult to believe, then, that many people who could earn much more by working would refuse to do so and prefer to collect public assistance. That there are a few who will so behave is quite possible; however, this would not justify working on the assumption that the majority behaves in this way. It is possible, however, that if they were permitted to work at wage rates below the present minimum and were not penalized, as they were till very recently and still are but to a lesser extent, by being taxed at nearly 100 percent rates (because of the proportional loss in public assistance as soon as income from work is earned) some of them might be able to try to find employment, though it is doubtful that it would be offered to them.

This might explain the lower than average labor force participation of some people of working age who are discouraged from seeking employment because none is available because of their partial or total unemployability. That most of those capable of working are already doing so is exemplified by the presence of approximately 5 million working poor in the labor force. This same view seems to be supported by some limited evidence collected by the Manpower Administration on the potential for work of welfare parents.[11]

It is important to recognize that if and when the government sets out to provide employment for the unemployed, it is influencing the allocation of scarce economic resources in very specific ways, particularly in the case where work is not entirely redundant in the sense that it does add to total production. This suggests that the values of the administration in question, or sheer expediency, would dictate production to some extent. Desirable as this might appear at times, it is in direct conflict with the basic tenets of market economics whereby the latter is allowed to function unhindered, except by accident. Besides, if their work is *not* totally redundant it would mean that market rehabilitation is the indicated policy and, therefore, guaranteed jobs have no justification. If their work is redundant, on the other hand, then one may ask what is the point in making people work for the sake of working. In the specific case of unemployed labor, structurally or cyclically, people would, in any event, be covered by unemployment insurance and, as indicated earlier, coverage should be universal to avoid that some people may be left out.

Those in the United States who would seem to welcome the guaranteed job approach appear to fall into two major, overlapping categories: the first group is comprised of people who prefer to see welfare recipients doing work even though production might not be enlarged. The idea of income without work is still alien to them.[e] They, of course, have not fully appreciated the value of manpower development in helping those who can benefit from it, not the inability of the market mechanism to absorb unemployables.

The second group is somewhat more academically oriented. Its members have come to the conclusion that the quality of life in America has been deteriorating rapidly, despite a significant gain in material wealth, and they would, in general, welcome increased government expenditures aimed at its improvement. Guaranteed employment may not, of course, be the only way to accomplish this, but it is certainly one way. It would provide that all those able to work should be employed by the government to take care of those activities as might improve the quality of life. Although the character of employment is more permanent, the idea does not differ significantly from the emergency public works established during the 1930s. The point they may be missing is that a well-functioning market economy—with adequate provisions against economic insecurity—would, in any case, be allocating its scarce economic resources in ways that reflect the wishes of its members. If the American people felt strongly that the quality of life in this country ought to be improved, they would find the market system their best ally in achieving this objective, or they would voluntarily allocate more resources to the government for such objectives as they think should be pursued. Failure occurs when market imperfections are allowed to impair the efficiency of the market mechanism, as when legislation exists that protects the very monopolistic practices that create environmental problems. If this group is concerned about these imperfections, then the solution lies in eliminating them, not in introducing new ones.

What the American people really need is adequate information on which to base their individual and collective decisions, not someone, such as the government, telling them what is good for them. Under present conditions, information would help offset market imperfections, however, it must be borne in mind that it is not a free commodity.

At this juncture, there are two relevant questions: first, how do the American people feel, in general terms, about these alternative solutions to the problem of economic insecurity? Second, what seems to be the prevailing attitude in Washington toward this issue? Of course, these two attitudes are not likely to be independent of each other.

In answer to the first question, it seems that the average taxpayer is more inclined toward the guaranteed job approach, probably because of what appears to him a saving, even if only in the short run. However, no concensus is yet in sight, probably because of the dearth of information concerning the effect of the various proposals. Only lately have serious attempts been made to estimate the possible cost of various programs, but this information has not yet filtered to the general public. Fears that the cost of alternate programs might be too high may have persuaded many a taxpayer to favor the guaranteed job. Also, many of

---

[e]It may be instructive to remind them that more and more the direct connection between wages and the value of production is becoming rather loose under the impact of automation and that this whole issue needs revision and further investigation.

them are not likely to envision themselves looking for jobs in the near future, particularly in view of the increased job security they have been able to acquire by various means. Finally, it is possible that the present state of the economy, with the influence of the Vietnam conflict, may be clouding their long-run vision of the issue.

Concerning the people on behalf of whom the final decision would have to be made, it is often heard that many of them tend to prefer the guaranteed job approach too. One can only wonder whether they fully appreciate what manpower development with the support of an adequate minimum guaranteed income might do for many who are potentially able to work. However, it is likely that theirs is a very short-run perspective, too, since they know, by experience, how difficult it would be to secure complete market rehabilitation under present commitments. Thus there is perhaps no major disagreement on the matter of principle and this is likely to influence Washington's attitude, as the recent wave of demands for the creation of government jobs attests. Some evidence does exist in support of the theory that the labor force participation rates of low income urban workers tend to be very sensitive to changing economic conditions—that is when economic conditions improve their labor force participation rates tend to rise. This may be viewed as lending some support to the belief that many of the people at the receiving end want to work rather than merely to receive a guaranteed income.[12] Higher labor force participation rates among non-white women, in general, point in the same direction. The withdrawal of some trainees from existing manpower development programs when a job becomes available is somewhat ambiguous evidence. It could be a positive desire to hold a job, but it could also reflect the quality of some of the programs, or that the financial support they are receiving is grossly inadequate.

It should be pointed out, however, that since these people are far from being a homogeneous group, some differences of opinion have developed on this subject. For one thing, not all of them are capable of working or of holding a job. Be that as it may, all this is an empirical matter which deserves the greatest consideration, at least much more than it has received thus far. It is important that the American people be made aware—whether they are at the receiving or at the giving end—of the significance and possible consequences of the alternatives open to them, and of what is involved in the social and economic rehabilitation of the economically unproductive group, so that they are in a better position to vote constructively on the matter.

With regard to the second question, the attitudes prevailing in Washington about the issue are in a constant state of flux. This reflects two factors: first, the differences in values among the various protagonists, and the lack of national concensus which, of course, is likely to affect Washington's position. Second, the changing character of the economy which tends to change minds regarding the order of priorities. Witness, for example, the effect that the current recession seems to have had on attitudes, particularly after such a relatively long period of prosperity.

It is worth noting that several commissions have studied the problem of economic insecurity and no doubt their recommendations carry some considerable weight. Among them are the 1966 Advisory Council on Public Welfare, the Arden House Conference on Public Welfare of 1967, the Advisory Commission on Intergovernmental Relations, and the very powerful Heineman Presidential Commission appointed by President Johnson which submitted its final recommendations to President Nixon in 1969.

At the political level efforts have been made to move on all fronts; to improve the American Social Security system to obviate the major criticisms referred to before, to try to institute guaranteed income and/or job programs, and to strengthen manpower development policies in order to tackle the problem at its roots, for there is insufficient commitment to any one of them, due to the inadequate knowledge. Complicating the picture is the latest move to operate through revenue-sharing and decentralized decision-making in some of these areas while standardizing the minimum assistance provided and the administration of some programs. This is an interesting possibility, but a paradoxical one given the American institutional framework. However, it is this multiple approach that slowly, but gradually, may develop into something closer to national concensus with regard to this complex issue.

Even at this stage, it is possible to point out some preferences as the debate progresses. The Presidential Commission has recommended a scale of assistance that would provide an impoverished family of four with a guaranteed $2,400 minimum annual income in cash. Table 4-2 below shows the structure of payments based on family size and amount of other income. The break-even level of income for a family of four has been set at $4,800 and the idea that economies of scale exist in family living has been built into the structure of payments.

The commission's recommendations do not require that recipients of this annual income seek work as a condition of eligibility, but they do provide some work incentive, since benefits decline by only 50 cents for each dollar of other income up to the break-even level. The commission has also tried to ensure that those who work receive higher incomes than those who do not, bearing in mind the peculiar case of the working poor. The commission's own estimate of the net cost of the program is approximately between $5 and $6 billion. (This figure might have to be revised upward if the current inflationary trend continues.) However, other estimates that consider variables like reduced tax base have come up with estimates ranging from $6 billion to $10 billion in additional costs to the federal government.[13]

President Nixon proposed to Congress a program that, in principle, is a guaranteed income scheme not too different from the commission's recommendations, but which still is a hybrid to some extent. It is more limited than the commission recommended, however, and geared to families with children only. A family of four with no earnings would receive $1,600 per year ($500 for the first two family members and $300 for each family member thereafter). It can go as high as $2,500 for a family of seven. A family of four with earnings of

Table 4-2
Proposed Schedule of Payments under the Presidential Commission on Income Maintenance Plan, by Size of Family and Other Sources of Income

Household size[a]	Amount of other income (in dollars)									
	0	500	1000	1500	2000	3000	4000	5000	6000	7000
One person	750	500	250	0						
One parent, one child	1200	950	700	450	200	0				
Couple	1500	1250	1000	750	500	0				
One parent, two children	1650	1400	1150	900	650	150	0			
Two parents, one child	1950	1700	1450	1200	950	450	0			
Four persons	2400	2150	1900	1650	1400	900	400	0		
Five persons	2850	2600	2350	2100	1850	1350	850	350	0	
Six persons	3300	3050	2800	2550	2300	1800	1300	800	300	0
Seven persons	3750	3500	3250	3000	2750	2250	1750	1250	750	250

[a]Households with four or more persons are assumed to have two adults.

Source: *Poverty Amid Plenty, The American Paradox*, The Report of the President's Commission on Income Maintenance Programs, U.S. Government Printing Office.

up to $3,920 per year is eligible for payments and the break-even level of income for a family of seven is $5,720. The first $720 of earnings are exempt and thereafter benefits are reduced by 50 percent up to the corresponding break-even level of income. This program is supposed to be supplemented with the Food Stamp Program which can raise the combined income (cash and kind) up to $2,464 in the case of a family of four with no earnings. The Nixon proposal has work requirements which are much in line with those under the 1967 Amendment to the Social Security Act, to be discussed later. The cost of the Nixon proposal has been estimated at an additional $5 billion plus $4 billion for existing programs since his proposal is much less divorced from the present system than is the Presidential Commission's proposal.[f]

It is perhaps understandable, politically speaking, that the Nixon Administration feels persuaded to work through the Food Stamp Program, since this program is currently in operation and it may make the task of getting his proposal through Congress easier, particularly since payments in kind are common within the present assistance structure. However, as a matter of economic and moral principle, this author wishes to go on record as opposing this approach vehemently. If people receive all of their income in cash, they will be able to signal to producers their preferences through the market mechanism.

[f]It is this author's belief that if the people of this country want this to be the limit of their commitment, then some sort of built-in automatic mechanism should, at least, be added so that these figures could be revised periodically in line with any economic progress made by the American economy.

It appears that underlying this whole philosophy of payments in kind is the idea quite unproven that low income people do not know how to spend their income. In the first place, there is some recent evidence that low income families tend to spend their incomes in very much the same fashion as people with higher incomes allowing for some differences in the relative importance of the various items.[14] It is logical that low income families, for example, spend relatively more money on rent. Second, it is anti-democratic for one group to impose its values on another group because the latter is in need. The old argument that some heads of family do not take proper care of their families suggests that the government should try to correct the problem when feasible, but it should not be used as an excuse to extend this mechanism to everyone who needs financial assistance. This is an issue of great significance for economic minorities for they are directly affected by such a policy. It is disappointing that such a prestigious group as the Committee for Economic Development has endorsed such a position, if only on a temporary basis.[15] Finally, it is very unfortunate that no provisions exist to assist those that do not have children.

The Nixon Administration's position is rather ambiguous regarding the guaranteed income-guaranteed job controversy. In the Manpower Revenue Sharing Act, the President is recommending public employment and public service job creation as part of an overall manpower program, although in principle, of a transitional and short-term nature. It is, however, possible to make out of the program either a place for training or a place where a job is guaranteed. If the former, there are better solutions than this one. If the latter, opposition to such schemes has already been explained. This ties in with the 1967 Amendment to the Social Security Act requiring training or work from welfare recipients. It can only be said the Administration seems to be confusing rehabilitation with anti-recession policies not clearly geared to retraining. This point is partially illustrated by the Nixon request (June 13, 1971) that the highest priority be given to an effective mobilization of federal resources to place the growing number of unemployed veterans.[16]

The pros and cons of the Presidential Commission and the Nixon recommendations cannot be discussed here, but they do suggest that the Administration has a certain predilection for some form of guaranteed income to be built into the American Social Security system, but that at present it is moving with caution, perhaps in order to attract support from as many quarters as possible, but also because of the lack of complete understanding of what is involved in this process. The result is a rather confusing picture, to say the least. Implicit in them, also, is the continuation of current efforts in the manpower development field and a realization, if only incipient, that a greater degree of integration between the two strategies is highly desirable.

Congress, on the other hand, seems to be somewhat more sympathetic to the idea of some form of guaranteed job supplemented by an active manpower development program. But its ideas appear somewhat mixed and it might be persuaded to switch to some form of guaranteed income as the composition of its membership changes and as new developments take place in the American economy. However, at present, the impact of the economic recession is still very much a factor. For example, a $5.5 billion economic development bill that includes a large public works program was passed by the Senate quite recently.[17] It authorizes $2 billion for projects such as the building of city halls, although Democrats claim it is an effort to create jobs for the poor. This illustrates the many forces at work and how unpredictable the position of Congress is at this point.

Still, the major operating device is the 1967 Amendment to the Social Security Act, whereby all those who do not accept work or training will be subject to the loss of financial assistance. Employment offices were instructed to arrange for the setting up of special projects to employ those who were found unsuitable for job training and those for whom no jobs could be found. By the same token, welfare agencies were instructed to make arrangements to insure child care whenever it might be required. The act provided for work incentive (WIN) in order to avoid the criticism of a 100 percent tax rate on the earnings of welfare recipients that existed in many states. Families with dependent children who receive financial aid (AFDC) can earn up to $30 from other sources without having to pay income taxes; but, they lose $2 out of every $3 they earn above the first $30; however youths attending school can earn any amount with no loss of welfare payments.

Unfortunately, under Aid to Families with Dependent Children—Unemployed Parents (AFDC-UP), many families do not qualify due to the limitations still existing on payments to unemployed parents. Implementation of this program seems to have moved slowly at first due to insufficient funds as well as variations in local-state laws concerning welfare and employment practices. But, it has been gaining some momentum and when carried out adequately, the program would represent a combination of manpower development, if embryonic in nature, and economic security through job training and guaranteed job, with a fringe of people (those exempt) receiving what is tantamount to a guaranteed income.

By the end of 1970, 260 WIN projects were in operation and enrollment totalled 218,000. The President has called for 187,000 first-time enrollees in WIN during the 1972 fiscal year compared with an estimated 125,000 for fiscal year 1971.[18] It is expected that eventually work registration will reach 2.5 million, including the 1.2 million working poor who would qualify under current welfare reform proposals.

It is still very vague what Congress actually intends in stating that jobs should be provided for those deemed unsuitable for retraining. Congress' idea of training seems to be merely to incorporate those who are considered trainable into already existing manpower development programs while no specific commitment has as yet been made in this area. This might turn out to be a very delicate matter, for many of these people actually require long-range economic and social rehabilitation for which existing manpower development programs might prove either unsuitable or inadequate, or both. As it stands, it seems possible that a person who is, in fact, socially and economically unemployable might be forced into taking a job—if necessary, provided by the government as an employer of last resort. This, if strictly enforced and literally interpreted, could result in some form of slave labor. This is an issue of the utmost significance for those who comprise the economic minority family, for many of them depend very much on long-range rehabilitation programs if they are to become truly productive.

One point needs to be raised before proceeding. Policies to expand school enrollment or to encourage people to stay in the armed forces could be very easily used as devices to tower unemployment—disguised guaranteed jobs schemes. The evidence is far from substantial that these policies are being used; however, it is a possibility that cannot be ruled out entirely, and it should be discouraged.

It appears that neither the Administration nor Congress looks upon their respective solutions to the problem of economic insecurity as superceding the present Social Security system, at least not in the foreseeable future. Rather they are expected to work through and supplement the working of the existing Social Security system. This is very much in the American tradition of doing things—not to do away with an old institution until the new one has proved its worth. Efforts are, however, being made to improve its performance by increasing coverage. For example, the Employment Security Amendments of 1970 ordered the extension of the unemployment insurance program to 5 million more workers by 1972. Also, they authorized a longer duration of unemployment benefits in times of high employment. Benefits for Social Security pensioneers were also increased recently and the House is seriously considering a rather significant escalation of the wage base to match rising wage levels, which will allow for much larger benefits upon retirement in the near future.[19]

It is this author's position that the provision of economic security, at least in an advanced industrial socio-economic system relying heavily on the market mechanism, should center around a well conceived manpower development base which can take care of the social and economic rehabilitation of anyone able to profit from it.[g] This should include long-range rehabilitation whenever it is deemed necessary. The latter is much needed in the United States today because of the existence of economic minorities who, in many instances, may require such long-range rehabilitation if a realistic attempt is to be made to improve drastically their relative position in this country's socio-economic structure. In the long run, this long-range rehabilitation would tend to become less important, for fewer people would be needing it, particularly if the problem is tackled at an early age. Moreover, this manpower development base would help to insure a more nearly balanced economy where the cost of economic trade offs would be greatly reduced, as was explained in the preceding section. This in itself would represent a major contribution to the struggle against economic insecurity, for it would reduce the adverse effect of economic dislocations which is one of the major sources of economic insecurity.

---

[g]Since this manpower development base should improve the performance of the market mechanism it would satisfy the underlying philosophy of this study.

This manpower development base should be adequately supplemented in two major ways: first, by a comprehensive Social Security program organized along the insurance principle. The extent of government participation in this program, however should be limited to the provision of just enough to prevent a worker and his family from falling into absolute poverty. Government participation would have to vary, then, with the type of economic insecurity, for not all of them pose the same threat to a family's standard of living. For example, the threat posed by premature death differs from that posed by temporary unemployment of the cyclical type, for the needs of the families are not necessarily the same. Government participation may also be necessary in those cases where private enterprise fails to respond to, or cannot come up with, a program to meet a specific need. This minimum, of course, should be realistic and adjustable automatically to take into account changes in the level of economic development of this country. Otherwise we are likely to have recurrent problems of inadequacy which eventually may render the mechanism unsatisfactory. Any additional protection above this minimum would have to be financed by each family through the market mechanism.[h] Of course, the amount of additional protection that a family wishes to purchase will tend to vary with the family's tastes and values and should be purchasable in competitive markets.

Dependency on fringe benefits should be deemphasized except to the extent that they are purchased with wages that are not monopolistically extracted and if they are so administered as not to prevent labor mobility. This social security program would serve to protect people who have been part of the labor market at one time or another and who find themselves threatened by economic insecurity, thus insuring that people who are able to work contribute to their own protection as much as possible. Social security functions, in this case, as an income maintenance device.

Second, this manpower development base should be supplemented by some form of guaranteed minimum income scheme to assist people who are beyond rehabilitation through the manpower development mechanism and who have not been part of the labor market. This guaranteed minimum income scheme might have to include a sub-program to supplement the earnings of people who are trainable from an economic point of view, but whose income from work might be considered socially inadequate. This is applicable, however, only if this category of workers is retained rather than phased-out completely, and should be looked upon as a transitional device. If and when manpower development programs are in full operation this group would have no reason to exist unless a very unrealistic social minimum income is established.

The possibility of setting an unrealistically high social minimum income is one which this author does not fear at the present stage of this country's social and economic development. No special provision on work incentive seems to be

---

[h]It appears that a minimum of protection provided through the government is something desirable in order to maintain the democratic process. This would reduce the possibility of some families being neglected to the point that they lack even a bare minimum of economic security; thereby, becoming extremely vulnerable to the incidence of poverty.

necessary in this approach to the problem of economic insecurity, but if society deems such a provision desirable it could be easily incorporated into it. For example, it could be used in the case of people who can be rehabilitated from an economic point of view but who cannot earn the socially determined minimum income if this group is retained as mentioned above. The supply of labor should be allowed to adjust, however, to this institutional framework and no specific effort should be entertained to force the labor supply into some predetermined pattern.

Finally, it should be pointed out that this approach does not need any special provision for the transitional income needs of people who have to undergo labor market rehabilitation for they are meant to be taken care of through either the social security program or the guaranteed income machinery or both as discussed above. The program ought to remain flexible enough to take into account any new form of economic insecurity.

The financing of the social security system should be done by those who benefit except in those cases where the production of the goods and services involves risks. In this case, the consumer should pay for it. It is possible that workers be allowed to contribute according to size of family and level of earnings. This, however, should be determined by society at large and can be easily incorporated into such a program. If economic change becomes too much of a burden and the latter happens to be unevenly distributed, the system may have to redistribute income not entirely at random, and some minimum base may even have to be financed from general taxes. This is an issue which does not affect the above recommendations in the immediate future, but which could be easily considered. For those who need permanent guaranteed incomes, a redistribution of income from the economically productive group will be absolutely necessary.

Finally, one point needs emphasis. Whether the final option is for social security or a guaranteed income program, or both, the level of income provided will have to be adequate—given the average standard of living of this country. At the beginning, the task may appear difficult to say the least, because the problems affecting economic minorities have not received adequate attention for many years and have been accumulating. However, eventually the task would become routine and manageable, as such programs become built into this nation's socio-economic system. With improved efficiency and high levels of productivity, the difficulties of the transitional period should not prove to be insurmountable.

5 Economic Minorities and Manpower Development

Thus far, this study has centered around an analysis of the strategic position manpower development should occupy in an industrially advanced, market-oriented economy, and on its role in laying down the foundations on which to build a workable system of economic security. The focus of analysis now shifts to the issue of economic minorities in manpower development, with particular reference to the American situation. There is no intention here to do away with the self-imposed market constraint, despite the nature of the problem. This may seem to pose a dilemma, but in fact, the opportunity to offer a solution is a challenge welcomed by this author, for it would enable him to attempt to dispel a serious misconception that has been plaguing the analysis of the problem of economic minorities.

The nature of the dilemma is as follows. On the one hand, economic minorities are, if anything, a marginal component of the labor force. Changes in the structure of the economy and/or the level of economic activity tend to affect them disproportionately under the present institutional framework. The former, in particular, seems to have become a more serious problem for it has tended to be accompanied by the need to upgrade labor quality. The problem is complicated by a rather strong tendency in the United States whereby people at the margin always tend to come from the same groups. This reflects the lack of equal access to economic opportunity that seems to prevail in the United States, a phenomenon that has become largely institutionalized. For example, in the educational system, if a person attends a school of below average standing, the cards are stacked against him relative to people that have been able to attend better schools. (This is particularly true if he wants to attend college.) If the root cause lay in an inherent lack of ability and/or willingness to do work, this situation would pose no basic problem. But in many cases the root cause lies not in the inherent shortcomings of the individual, but in discrimination of one kind or another.[a]

Even in the case of relatively less motivation, the possibility that this results from the institutionalization of this lack of equal access to economic opportunity cannot be ruled out completely. This should not be used, however, as a blanket justification whenever inadequate motivation is found. Of course, those attending low quality schools usually do not do so of their own free choice, but

---

[a]Whether discrimination is a more serious problem in this country than in others is not relevant to this study. This author does not in fact think so, for discrimination may take many different and subtle forms. The concern of this study is only with the fact that it does exist and that this has definite implications for the effective operation of the market system.

are forced into it by the present mechanism through which elementary and secondary schooling is financed in the United States, whereby property taxes are the most important source of financial support. This suggests that wealthier communities tend to have better schools, whereas poor communities, particularly those in overpopulated districts, tend to have relatively inferior schools due to inadequate financial means.

Given the present institutional framework, it appears that once a person falls into this category, it is very hard for him to get out of it. On the other hand, the market mechanism, in its allocation of resources, has to place some workers at the margin. This would occur whether equal access to economic opportunity were present or not. The solution to the dilemma consists precisely in using manpower development as a means of compensating for—and eventually putting an end to—this lack of access to equal opportunity. The equalization of economic opportunity is essential to the effective working of the market system. Therefore, there is no inconsistency in trying to assist economic minorities within the framework of the market system. Any inconsistency that might appear to exist at first is due to lack of understanding of what is involved in the functioning of the market mechanism. This need for equalization of economic opportunity is even greater in an industrial environment, for the problems which failure create here tend to become perpetuated and are more intractable.

Manpower development can be very useful in the struggle to rehabilitate economic minorities as a group, a group that still is quite large and whose members have increasingly become worse off in relative terms amid the increased prosperity enjoyed in the United States. The Interagency Manpower Planning Task Force estimated in 1968 that some 11 million people needed training. This is likely to underestimate the need for training because of inherent difficulties in estimating such a problem; for example, reduced labor force participation as an adjustment mechanism as in the case of early retirement. Besides, there is a growing number of people who currently do not seem to need training, but who are likely to need some in the immediate future to keep their jobs or find new ones. It is not clear to what extent the above estimate takes into account that many of these people need complete rehabilitation and not merely job training. At any rate, even this figure is impressive.

Certainly, even if manpower development could help everyone—and there is no evidence that it cannot help most people—the possibility always exists of some workers becoming members of the marginal group. But the cards need not be stacked against any specific group or groups. It should be simply a random event. Moreover, the term "economic minority" would not have to carry with it the connotation of absolute poverty if an effective system of manpower development rehabilitation, supplemented by an adequate system of income maintenance, were available and open to everyone on equal terms. The only thing manpower development cannot help to eliminate is relative poverty.

The major objective of manpower development with regard to economic minorities, therefore, is the equalization of economic opportunity, and this is quite in line with the major philosophy underlying this work. Whatever disagreement exists—and some legitimate differences are likely to arise—is concerned with how effective certain manpower development policies might be in equalizing economic opportunity and access to the market place. This, important as it is, is an empirical matter.

Manpower development as a tool to fight unemployment, particularly of the structural type, is of the utmost interest to economic minorities for it turns out to be a tool against poverty. It is the close association which exists between economic minorities and poverty that is so relevant here. Earlier in this study, it was noted that the unemployment rate was much higher among those groups where economic minorities tend to be heavily concentrated, since there is more than just cyclical unemployment affecting those figures. Unemployment, of course, is not the only means by which people become poverty-stricken, but it is certainly a major source of poverty in the United States. As Eli Ginzberg has so forcefully stated: "The transition from unemployment to poverty is gradual but often unavoidable."[1] This is true, at least, in the present stage of development of our means of providing economic security in the United States.

It is very significant to note that in the proposed Manpower Revenue Sharing Act there is a recommendation for an automatic trigger which would make more funds available for manpower development when the level of unemployment rises above a predetermined point.[b] Apart from the anticyclical characteristic that this policy may have, the important point is that it would obviate the reduction of such funds when there is a recession—a reduction that usually hurts economic minorities the most, and which may destroy any previous effort for rehabilitation—as well as possibly minimizing any possible adverse effect resulting from the interaction of structural and demand unemployment as discussed before. This policy would probably benefit other groups besides economic minorities which may make it politically more attractive.

Manpower development seems to be the only way to increase the average productivity of the working poor so that they do not have to depend on income supplements in order to emerge from a state of economic and social poverty. The working poor represent not only a very special case of unemployment, but one that has been growing in relative importance. If the American economy keeps on growing as it has, and nothing is done about this group and their descendents, the number of working poor would most likely continue to rise. For lack of a better term, society calls them "socially unemployed" for they are not equipped to earn an income from work which would place them above the income level considered a socially desirable minimum by present American standards. Yet, these socially unemployed are for the most part eager to go out to work, often under quite adverse conditions and regardless of their low earnings. Dorothy Newman recently has pointed out that the plight of the average working poor in America seems to be sometimes worse than that of

---

[b]It is not the intention here to debate the merits of this policy with reference to previous recommendations on manpower development. The only issue to raise, as long as that kind of policy might be instituted, is that any unemployment figure at the aggregate level is likely to be quite misleading for policy purposes.

many unemployed workers.[2] Her evidence also suggests that only 4 percent of all heads of poor families in the labor force were actually unemployed in 1966—unemployed in the sense of having no job at all. Quite often they are not protected by the existing social insurance machinery, and when they turn to the public assistance system, they are still, in many states, ineligible for benefits. This is an interesting paradox, for society is, in fact, penalizing people who are willing to work; yet some people seem to think the poor are not willing to work, as the current barrage of work requirement proposals would indicate.

Information about the situation of the working poor has served considerably to enlighten the American people with regard to the problem of economic minorities. It has helped to show that working is not a sufficient insurance against poverty and income insecurity and, therefore, poverty does not necessarily imply laziness or lack of character. Raising minimum wages usually hurts the working poor, if only in the short-run. This would not be too serious if they could count on some form of income maintenance device. Displacement without upgrading of his skill leaves the worker with little prospect of finding another job. Retraining has not been always effective in lifting the working poor out of poverty, for it has very seldom encompassed the idea of total rehabilitation. Usually, it means a job with perhaps some greater stability of employment—no doubt an improvement but not a lasting solution to the problem. If and when some form of guaranteed minimum income comes into existence—like the Nixon proposal—the work incentive provision may help the working poor to keep some of both incomes (the guaranteed one and the income from work); however, this would not provide a permanent solution to the problem either, although it would alleviate poverty.

Finally, manpower development can combat poverty by assisting several members of a family to enter the labor market. While many are ill-equipped to compete successfully in the labor market, for some it may only be a question of lack of adequate supporting services, for example, the availability of day care centers. The fact that so many of them are willing to enter the labor market, if only temporarily, when jobs are relatively abundant, suggests the potential of manpower development in this area. The expansion of sectors of the economy where part-time employment and flexible hours of work can be arranged may be of some value in making this possible. Many families living in poverty today might be able to improve their relative financial position considerably by simply having more than one member of the family earning income from work. But, in order to do this they are likely to need some preparation. Borrowing Ornati's concept of poverty bands, many of these people could, in this way, move at least from a level of minimum subsistence to one of minimum adequacy of minimum comfort.[3]

The idea of economic and social rehabilitation seems to be at times a difficult one to comprehend for people who have never needed it. Although not all economic minorities may need it, many do, particularly those economic minorities who tend to be culturally handicapped and are usually associated with the ghetto-slum type of residence. That adjustment to the requirements of the broader industrial society of which they are part, if only nominally sometimes, is a difficult endeavor is demonstrated by the frequently reported adjustment problems of agricultural labor to industrial life, particularly in an urban setting. Notice that this adjustment has been difficult even when the people involved have been rather well integrated into the American culture. Equipping people for this adjustment should start at elementary and secondary school level; for those who have passed that age, the task is bound to be more complex. Members of economic minorities are no exception to this problem and the longer they have been economic minorities, the more difficult is the challenge.

Social and economic rehabilitation means not only properly equipping members of economic minorities to enter the market economy as producers but also incorporating them into the mainstream of American life, that is into the mainstream of our highly urbanized and industrialized advanced society so they can function effectively. Otherwise, any progress made in bringing them temporarily into the production process may go to waste, for all this is an integral process. (This has been particularly difficult for some groups to achieve because of the obstacles put in their way.) Those who cannot succeed in entering the mainstream tend to withdraw from society, at least partially. That this is a time-consuming process is clear, too; but it is equally clear that it is long overdue. This author also concedes that it is an expensive proposition, but this should not be used as an excuse for not starting somewhere, especially since it will facilitate a more orderly expansion of the economy as well as a more efficient allocation of resources. This obviously is a long-term process, but it promises to be more effective than just short-run retraining where the results may be temporary and in the long-run frustrating for those involved, not to mention costly. One thing is certain: to get people to participate, it is necessary to indicate to them a long-term commitment of resources in order to dispel the idea that funds may be cut at any moment. This, of course, requires the commitment of this nation. Without such a national commitment, no administration can plan and implement such long-range rehabilitation, because of the need to justify performance every four years.

Even the best organized manpower development effort to assist economic minorities would not benefit everyone equally. Age is probably the most important variable in this respect. After all manpower development is largely an investment in human capital, and this means youngsters are the ones who stand to benefit the most. However, assisting their parents today may prove a very effective way of helping the children in economic minorities to be better equipped to enter the labor market tomorrow. Where a certain culture of poverty has developed, doing away with it is essential in helping children over the long-run. As it has been so persuasively stated:

"If it be true that the children of the poor today are themselves destined to be the impoverished parents of tomorrow, then some social intervention is needed to break the cycle, to interrupt the circuits of hunger and hopelessness that link generation to generation."[4]

Rehabilitation of the young is important too, because they still have their entire working life ahead of them. With regard to age, one of the most difficult challenges is in helping those who have been forced to withdraw from the labor force early in life. In a recent study by the Bureau of Labor Statistics, it was found that between 1962 and 1965, most of the decline in labor force participation of the age group 55-64 was among those with the lowest education.[5] Considerable time should go to the development of suitable means of assisting those over 45 years of age who need retraining or rehabilitation, for their age is a factor against them and yet they have quite a few years to go before retirement.

The general tendency today is to center manpower development programs for the coming generation around education.[c] Very little is known as to what might be the most effective educational alternatives this country can offer its youth, particularly those who come from economic minorities, though some experimentation is currently underway. The evidence on school dropouts usually suggests serious drawbacks in the educational system, particularly for economic minorities, since this group comprises a higher percentage of dropouts.

That school dropouts pose a serious challenge for manpower development is suggested by a recent study of the Bureau of Labor Statistics in which it was found that whether measured by unemployment rates, earnings, or steadiness of employment, the record of school dropouts compares very unfavorably with that of those who were able to finish high school.[6] Among the solutions advanced and that seem promising is that of erecting bridges between the worlds of school and work. The experience of other countries should be explored, but care should be exercised in interpretation, because of possible differences in socio-economic systems. Helping school dropouts is extremely important, because they are good candidates for the working poor of tomorrow, or even worse, complete dependents upon public assistance.

One of the most disheartening aspects of the problem of education is the inadequate knowledge that exists concerning the proper relationship between technological change and the educational system. This is a subject that requires the most intensive and extensive kind of research. As pointed out by Bright:

"It is important that we understand how man-machine relationships are changing, since we are basing educational plans, retraining programs, union agreements, wage policies and social legislation and even attitudes upon this relationship."[7]

Given this inadequate knowledge and the prevailing uncertainty, the leaning seems to be toward the provision of a reasonably well-rounded education. It

[c]This study is not the place to discuss what might be the best way to assist economic minorities through the educational system, nor does such a discussion lie within the author's area of competence. Moreover, the entire American educational system is currently under attack and may undergo considerable change before long. Increasingly, the feeling is that it does not reflect the needs of our time, though no one seems able to define, with precision, what those needs are.

appears that in those instances where a more specialized training is considered necessary, the emphasis should be on theory as much as possible since this would enable the individual to encompass new and more advanced developments in his area of competence. There seems to be some evidence suggesting that students who do not receive a well-balanced education tend to become poorly motivated and potential underachievers.[8]

In the case of economic minorities, some experimentation is under way in the area of curriculum development and teaching techniques to aid this group. This includes the development of programs where vocational and academic training are combined to make the return to school for dropouts easier, particularly now that it is sometimes possible to assist them financially while attending school. At least, there is a greater realization that traditional methods of teaching are quite often of little value in dealing with people who do not have a middle class background. The learning process requires values and study habits which members of economic minorities do not always possess, however, it may be feasible to adjust the learning process better to their needs.

A very delicate and complex issue is that of deciding how much manpower development is to be made available to economic minorities, free of charge. While manpower development undoubtedly is an investment from which the individual can reap the benefits, it is also essential to recognize that economic minorities lack the means to avail themselves of such services. If they could, they would not be economic minorities. If and when this society decides to phase out absolute poverty and provide a minimum of economic security, it will have to pay for that investment. This investment is, however, largely self-financing from a long-run point of view, for it is more than likely that it will increase productivity, and in so doing, increase the tax base. However, the major justification is that this manpower development, in the case of economic minorities, is the principal way of more nearly equalizing access to economic opportunity. Finally, and on more practical grounds, the social benefits accruing from this investment are more than likely to be greater than the private benefits it yields; this justifies, at least, some subsidization.

Manpower development is not only capable of increasing productivity, but it can also alter the present, as well as the future, income distribution of this country: the former through direct subsidization of the program, the latter through a relatively greater participation of economic minorities in future productivity gains. Schultz has made it abundantly clear that the current structure of earnings reflects, to a very considerable extent, the distribution of investment in human capital. This suggests that the provision of manpower development for economic minorities, if provided free until a more nearly equal access to economic opportunity exists, can redistribute income toward this group. At a future date, as this investment starts to bear fruit, this group might be able to improve their relative position in the structure of earnings, or even participate, for the first time, in some instances. This is not in contradiction with the underlying philosophy of this study, for the restoration of such an environment is essential to it and is long overdue.

Last, but by no means least, if society chooses to accelerate its rate of economic progress, a heavier burden will tend to be imposed on the marginal component of the work force; this may require a distribution of the burden on a more nearly equal basis. This is likely to mean subsidization of manpower development programs for those so affected—the economic minorities of today, or those of tomorrow.

In deciding upon the amount of manpower development to be offered free, a serious difficulty is bound to arise. Sometimes, it is hard to separate the investment aspect of a given manpower development policy from any consumption aspect it might have. In this connection, the most difficult case seems to be that of education. Education is, beyond any doubt, consumption (present and future) and investment at the same time. Unfortunately, students of this problem have not yet been able to produce a satisfactory method of measuring how much it is one and how much the other, and it is seriously doubted if they ever will. There seems to be a concensus regarding a socially dictated minimum of consumption education that this country would like to provide to everyone, and it is important that economic minorities should not be excluded from this. But, the fact is that they would have to be given relatively a greater amount of this type of education if they were to be brought into the mainstream of American life at the earliest possible date. As for the investment side of education, it is important to determine how much education of this type economic minorities must have to become competitive on an equal opportunity basis. Above and beyond this amount, the issue becomes extremely controversial.

It would appear desirable to establish a system of loans to which economic minorities would have full access. A loan system seems to be appropriate in a market-oriented economy, because once access to economic opportunity has been equalized, there is no justification for free investment education. After all, this investment education should enhance the ability of its recipient to earn an income. In an advanced industrial society the burden of providing that education from which a person can profit substantially should not be imposed on the family, for in a system of free markets this would be a very heavy burden. The need for a subsidy here would only arise where it can be shown that the social benefits from this investment exceed its private benefits. The subsidy should be sufficient to cover only the difference between the social and the private benefit. In principle, it would seem justifiable to charge the cost of the subsidy to the people who seem to benefit, even if not directly, from this investment. However, in practice there is a tendency for society as a whole to pay for it through taxes, because of the many difficulties associated with the identification not only of the benefits but also of their recipients. This is an issue that deserves much more consideration than it is currently receiving. In the case of economic minorities, however, the amount of investment that would have to be provided free to them is so considerable at this point that, for some time, the issue will tend to be largely academic.

The issue of who actually pays for manpower development should not be taken lightly, for sometimes economic minorities tend to pay not only for their own manpower development, but also for that of others. When this occurs, manpower development is redistributing income in a perverse way. This tends to reflect the existing tax structure and the extent to which the various income groups have access to manpower development. The greater the relative participation of economic minorities in manpower development program, the less likely this is to occur.

It should be borne in mind that the working poor do pay taxes. The lowest tax rate on taxable income is 14 percent, so even if only part of their income is subject to such a rate, it is already high enough, given their economic condition. This is a very important factor if income supplements are finally paid to this group. The Social Security tax is a much more debatable issue for this tax is applied to the purchase of some amount of economic security and, as recommended in the previous section, in general this tax should be borne by those who receive the benefits. As suggested by J.A. Brittain in a recent article, the tax (employee-employer contribution) can go as high as, for example, 12 percent in the case of a family of six with an income of $5,000 if, as he thinks, employers tend to shift this cost to the workers.[9] But even if employers could not shift this cost, workers will still be contributing a significant proportion of the tax payment. A case could be made either to take this tax payment into account when setting up the payment structure of any guaranteed minimum income scheme, or to pay the tax on their behalf through the program as long as they qualify for benefits. To the extent that state and locally financed programs exist, the burden on the poor may be even greater due to the heavier reliance of these governmental units on sales taxation and, in general, a less progressive structure of income taxes.

The phenomenon of economic minorities transferring income to non-economic minorities through manpower development is illustrated by the case of public higher education, at least in some cases. Professor W. Lee Hansen recently reported that the California public system of higher education might be redistributing income toward students who, for the most part, do not come from economic minorities; yet the latter do contribute taxes.[10] This seems to be a reflection of the variation in the level of subsidies by type of institution, admission policies, and the tax structure by which higher education is financed.

This author has recently found that the State University of New York (SUNY) system may be redistributing income in a perverse way, too, although this is partially mitigated by the setting up of special programs for the disadvantaged and a significant network of community colleges within reasonable distance of major urban centers, as well as the guarantee of a certain number of places on a country basis, a policy that sometimes benefits economic minorities. At any rate, low income students seem to be receiving relatively less than they contribute to SUNY. This author would like to go on record as saying that if public higher education—as a manpower development tool—is to redistribute current income, it should rather be toward economic minorities. However, the issue of whether public higher education should be used to redistribute current income or not, is beyond the scope of this study. The point to stress is the power of manpower development not only to equip economic minorities to enter the labor market but also to redistribute income, current as well as future, if so desired. The future structure of earnings of this country should reflect the effects of manpower development programs on economic minorities.

And in concluding, manpower development services in the United States have often been provided free to people who are not members of economic minorities. It is difficult to say whether or not this has been done on the assumption that the social benefits are greater than those to the individual, to the point that no charge should be made. If this has not been the justification, then these subsidies might be in conflict with the effective operation of the market system. Be that as it may, any such privileges that might be extended to groups, other than economic minorities, would have to be given in even greater amounts to economic minorities, or the principle of equalization of access to economic opportunity would not be upheld.

6

Economic Minorities in the Manpower Development Revolution

In this section, the implications for economic minorities of the 1960s legislative revolution in the manpower development field will be explored. The second, but related, objective will be to help determine how much progress may have been made in establishing the foundations for a comprehensive manpower development strategy, including the socio-economic rehabilitation of economic minorities as one of its leading priorities, if not as its foremost priority. Assisting economic minorities and establishing the foundations of a comprehensive manpower development ought to be the two most significant objectives of any such legislative revolution in the American case. No specific attempt has been made to analyze in detail its effectiveness, because this legislative effort still is very much in its experimental stages and has been subject to the political demands and expediencies of the 1960s, rather than to the exclusive needs of the people affected. While discussing the nature of the various programs, it should become apparent, at least in principle, whether or not they are in line with the underlying philosophy of this study. Their possible potential in helping to meet the above two objectives may also become clear.

Manpower policies of one kind or another have always existed in this country, even if sometimes by default. Agricultural extension programs, public education, immigration policies and the military services are some illustrations of active manpower policies. The major difference, as compared with what has taken place in recent years in this area, probably is they were not associated with a manpower development strategy, nor with any feeling of urgency, and that they were usually related to specific national objectives and only rarely directed primarily to the better utilization and conservation of human resources.

The American economy seems to have undergone some significant structural changes during the 1950s and early 1960s as the evidence introduced earlier suggests. These changes tended to be rather localized in nature, hence the unemployment they caused took, to a considerable extent, the form of pockets of unemployment. These, in turn, degenerated into pockets of poverty. The imperfect nature of the American market system coupled with some serious deficiencies in the manpower development field—for example, lack of adequate labor market information—were adding fuel to the flames. It is not surprising then that one of the earliest legislative attempts in the manpower development field during this era—the Area Redevelopment Act (ARA) of 1961—was directed to the solution of this problem. Its major concern was the retraining of workers affected by this kind of localized structural unemployment whose skills had either become obsolete or suffered a major decline in demand. This, it was expected, would make the areas affected by change in the structure of the economy relatively more attractive to industry, particularly because it was accompanied by a system of loans to help develop the economic infrastructure of the regions involved.

In principle, retraining can help to prepare workers for successful outmigration, too, particularly if it is not too specific in nature. This was not the intention of the ARA, however. It was not the primary objective of ARA to aid economic minorities. Nevertheless, it could be viewed as a preventive measure against enlargement of the ranks of the economic minority base of this country, because many of the families involved, if left unassisted, would eventually have become full partners of those already a part of the so-called culture of poverty. As previously noted, the transition from long-term unemployment to poverty is just a matter of time if no attempt is made to provide a minimum amount of economic security.

In 1962, the Trade Expansion Act (TEA) was passed. It was designed to help workers whose jobs become threatened by changes in the pattern of foreign trade. It was intended to support the decision of this country during the early 1960s to move toward trade liberalization. This suggests a case where policies directed to the expansion of production and employment may give rise to structural changes. The manpower development implications of the TEA are very similar to those of the ARA—it even has a loan feature to encourage modernization of production. In fact, the major type of unemployment problem that a movement toward trade liberalization might pose is where the temporary unemployment it causes turns out to be highly localized. Hence, it is possible to view the manpower component of the TEA as making provisions for cases similar to those involved in the ARA. It is anticipated that during 1971, great use will be made of the provisions of the act to assist workers affected by changes in foreign trade.[1]

The two acts seem to have made two major contributions toward the establishment of a manpower development strategy in the United States. First, they highlighted the need for positive manpower development action whenever the economy is subject to profound structural changes, if the transition is to be a smooth one and not arouse bitter opposition. By such action, the burden can be distributed somewhat more evenly. In this way, it can facilitate the restoration of intersectoral balances with a minimum of friction.

Second, the acts served to advance the idea of providing financial assistance for families whose breadwinners are undergoing labor market rehabilitation—a rather novel idea in the United States. A training allowance amounts simply to a form of income maintenance.

A third contribution could be added. This legislation suggested to the American people that the problem they were attempting to solve was a national one with very serious social, political, and economic ramifications. It also suggested, at least to some extent, that if some form of social intervention is necessary to speed the adjustment in the market mechanism—because this is considered socially desirable—the most effective way to do it is to channel such an effort through the market system.

The year 1962 also witnessed the passage of the Manpower Development and Training Act (MDTA). This is considered to be the major federal manpower development tool to combat unemployment in the United States, particularly of the structural kind. As originally conceived, it was designed to retrain workers whose skills had become, or were threatening to become, obsolete. However, through successive legislative amendments and agency interpretation the act has undergone some rather substantial evolution, thus it has become a more flexible instrument which can be used for manpower development in general.[2]

Some aspects of this evolution can best be understood in the light of some of the progress made on other fronts; for example, the War on Poverty, since the work done under this act has tended to become pivotal to that of other programs, particularly with regard to training. Nevertheless, its major responsibility still is training and retraining, including that which used to be conducted under the ARA.

Considerable progress has been made with regard to training allowances, including the defraying of costs such as transportation. Also, some significant progress has been achieved in allowing people collecting unemployment insurance to participate through special arrangements with the state agencies involved. This cooperation is very significant, for otherwise it would have been very difficult to get unemployed workers collecting unemployment compensation to participate in retraining. These measures to assure some fairly adequate income during retraining are of major interest to economic minorities, for quite often they are forced to interrupt or terminate their training to accept a job, due to inadequate income provisions. This results not only in a loss to those involved, but also in a loss to society because public money has been expended unproductively; yet the problem has not been eliminated.

In its original form, the MDTA had no specific provisions to assist economic minorities and reaching this group has required sometimes a special effort and expertise not available at its inception. This poses a problem, for it has to be recognized that economic minorities are generally at a disadvantage in relation to other groups. With relatively high levels of unemployment—not always structural—and with a very limited number of training slots available, economic minorities were left out to a considerable extent.

It has been estimated that at least 11 million people need some form of retraining. The total number of first-time enrollees under retraining programs in federally-sponsored programs, however, has not exceeded the 2 million mark, and this includes many people who have not really been receiving training. As a result of the evolution undergone by the MDTA, this policy was revised and by 1966 Congress had ordered that 65 percent of the trainees were to be drawn from disadvantaged groups with the other 35 percent of the training slots to be used to reduce labor shortages. This Congressional decision suggests a fundamental misunderstanding of manpower development, at least at that time. These two objectives—training the disadvantaged and reducing labor shortages—are far from mutually exclusive objectives. Labor shortages can be alleviated by training economic minorities. Of course, it is understood that not all members of this group can be trained over a short period of time, but, in principle, the distinction is unnecessary.[a]

The MDT program has three major components. In principle, they could be adjusted to assist economic minorities, but, in practice, some components are more suitable for this purpose than others. The first major component is an on-the-job training feature (OJT). This one is relatively less suitable to aid economic minorities, particularly those who are culturally handicapped. It requires good working habits, discipline and some experience on the part of the workers. The very idea of OJT is short-run in nature. This does not mean that economic minorities could not profit from it, but they are at a competitive disadvantage with respect to other would-be candidates. Since economic minorities are not a homogeneous group OJT might prove of some value to those of its members who are relatively better equipped to compete in the labor market.

OJT has a relatively low cost per trainee. For example, in 1965 its average cost per enrollee was approximately $500 as compared to $1,500 under institutional training.[3] It also tends to return workers to active work comparatively quickly. This latter feature is particularly attractive to economic minorities as long as inadequate income supplements exist to assist them. These are distinct advantages that have proved very attractive to Congress. As can be seen in table 6-1, Congress encouraged its expansion at the expense of institutional

Table 6-1
First-time Enrollment in MDT Programs

	(in thousands)		
	Institutional Training	OJT Program	Column 2 as a % of Column 1
1963	32	2	6.2
1964	69	9	13.0
1965	145	12	8.2
1966	177	58	32.7
1967	150	115	76.6
1968	140	101	72.1
1969	135	85	62.9
1970	130	91	70.0
Total	978	473	48.3
1971 (projected)	152	30	19.7

Source: *Manpower Report of the President*, 1971.

[a]It should be noted that Congress' definition of disadvantaged is not exactly the definition of economic minority used in this study, but for the purpose of the present analysis, the differences can be disregarded. Congress considers disadvantaged the following groups: under 22 years of age, over 44 years of age, non-white, high school not completed, rural residence and unemployed 15 weeks and over.

training since this meant helping more people for a given amount of expenditure which was politically enticing. The problem was that it could not reach very far into the economic minority family.

Recently, some attempts have been made to give economic minorities a greater opportunity in this program, by increasing the size of the average subsidy paid to private employers. This has resulted in a situation where, in a few instances, the cost per enrollee was higher in this program than the average cost under institutional training. This suggests that the nature of the people involved is a key factor in affecting costs, as should have been expected. This expansion has also been achieved through an increased partnership with Job Opportunities in the Business Sector (JOBS), to be discussed later. If the subsidy is intended to make up for the initial lower productivity of these workers it would be necessary to show evidence that the employers were not planning to hire them anyhow. Otherwise the program would be subsidizing private production, something that would be in direct conflict with the basic tenets of market economics, and indeed, quite uncalled for. The fact that the relative importance of the program within the MDT program has fluctuated with the business cycle, being higher during peak periods, hints at this possibility, though it is not sufficient evidence due to the changing nature of the program.

Finally, an effort would have to be made to prevent the program from drifting into some form of disguised guaranteed job program, unless this were its real purpose. If the latter were the intention it should be so stated.

The second major component of the MDT program is an institutional training feature. This is usually carried out in skill centers where basic education and vocational training are combined, including a multioccupational approach to find the most suitable combination for those involved. This component of the MDT program is, in principle, much more suitable in assisting economic minorities, for its encompasses—if only embryonically, so far—the idea of rehabilitation. It recognizes the need to provide prevocational and general supporting services to equip economic minorities to enter the job market with a reasonable chance of success.

The average cost per trainee in institutional training is much higher than in OJT, as noted earlier, but only when the latter does not involve any attempt to reach out for the most difficult to train economic minorities, that is the truly disadvantaged, culturally speaking. Considerable experimentation is under way to try to establish the right kinds of curricula to assist people in this program. In both programs, an effort has been made, not always successfully, to train people for occupations with some future. The relatively short period of time available for rehabilitation is a serious handicap in any such attempt.

The third major component of the MDT program is the Experimental and Demonstration (E&D) feature. As its name suggests, this is the experimental and research arm of the entire program. The contribution of this part of the program is far greater than might appear. It is sufficient to bear in mind how little was known at its inception on the best approaches to manpower development in the United States. At least in principle, it can serve to develop and test new ways to help in the social and economic rehabilitation of economic minorities. The contribution that this feature of the program can make in advancing the cause of economic minorities is also greater when its work is viewed against the backdrop of the War on Poverty through which many of these people can be located and assisted in various ways. Some of the programs in this category were instituted by administrative fiat, which was done through a very liberal interpretation of the act.

There is one interpretation of the role of E&D programs which warrants some consideration. It has been said that E&D programs should emphasize the building of manpower programs around the needs of the individual rather than around the needs of the job market.[4] This interpretation seems to be based on a misconception of the purpose of manpower development in a market economy. The emphasis throughout most of this study has been that the chief purpose of manpower development in such an economy is to make people more competitive in the labor market. This does not mean that the needs of the individual involved cannot be taken into account, but not in the sense of superseding or interfering with the performance of the labor market. To do the latter would be self-defeating. However, if what proponents of this view have in mind is merely that new ways of reaching economic minorities outside existing conventional patterns should be developed, they are probably right. But, this should be clearly stated.[b]

In 1963, the Vocational Education Act (VEA) was passed. It was the first major congressional attempt to revise American policy in the vocational training area in almost 50 years. Though still placing much of the emphasis on agricultural and home economic vocational training, some limited progress was made to expand vocational training in other directions. Table A-16 shows that in 1964, agricultural and home economics vocational training accounted for 18.8 percent and 44.3 percent respectively of the total enrollment, and that by 1969 their respective shares had declined to 10.7 percent and 30.7 percent, a significant drop indeed considering that the program was increasing rapidly in general.

However, while agricultural vocational training declined in absolute terms, too, home economics did not. The 1968 amendment to the act emphasizes the need for an even greater effort to relate vocational training to current job market conditions. This will probably allow the past trend of expanding training in new fields to continue since there are quite a few promising fields where sophisticated vocational training appears to be currently needed, especially in view of the imperfections that exist in the market and that make entry into some of these fields difficult. Limited as it is, vocational education legislation in general has represented probably the only direct bridge between the school system and the labor market that this country has had for years, although other links are now being forged under the influence of the MDT and related programs.

Currently being explored also is the possibility of providing some vocational education in elementary schools. This expansion in vocational education,

bOne particular E&D Program, the Labor Mobility experimental program, will be given considerable attention in the second part of this study.

particularly toward more promising fields, is important for the children of economic minorities, since it will still take some time before they can overcome disadvantages that make their entry into college difficult. Under conditions of rapid technological change, as well as of changes in the labor market, its significance should be subject to greater scrutiny by those in charge of the American educational system. At the very least, some streamlining, not only of programs but also in philosophy, of the American vocational educational system seems highly desirable.

Perhaps a closer integration with other job training programs might be advantageous. This program, in principle, holds some hope in assisting school dropouts in any successful bid to enter the labor market better equipped. This program has not been particularly designed to aid economic minorities as such. However, the more the agricultural and home economic aspects of the program are de-emphasized, the more the program could be designed to assist economic minorities, since more resources would be available to develop the aspects of the program which might be better suited to meet the needs of economic minorities. The 1968 Amendment does specifically refer to the disadvantaged and author-izes increased expenditures to assist them—another program where a shift in emphasis has taken place, if only to a limited extent so far.

In 1958, the National Defense Education Act (NDEA) was passed, amended subsequently in 1965. The original intent of the act was to help protect the international competitive advantage of the United States in the generation and application of knowledge, a central problem in the development of a strong human resource base. This program affects, and is affected by, labor market conditions, but its major concern does not rest always with the needs of the market. Given certain non-market goals—like national defense—this program might try, at times, to influence the labor market in specific directions, for example, by trying to increase the supply of high level manpower so that at each and every possible salary level more such talent will be offered.

The free interplay of the forces of supply and demand can always determine a price at which the market for particular skills could be cleared. However, given these non-market objectives, the price may be considered too high. The act has also been of some value in alleviating the shortages—in the above sense—of teachers, caused by the sudden but not unexpected influx of youngsters first into high school and later into college that occurred during the late 1950s and early 1960s. The fact that subsidies seem to have been relatively effective in increasing supply by reducing the cost side of obtaining a given income from work strongly suggests the power of the market mechanism in reshuffling resources when allowed to do so. But, in this instance it could equally have been achieved through the salary side.

The NDEA, though not having economic minorities as its primary target, has tended to serve them over the long-run. The problem of identifying the benefits that are accruing to economic minorities is that they are, for the most part, indirect benefits. In this connection its major contribution has come probably through the contribution of this program to the growth of the American economy, including here its contribution to the upgrading of the American educational system. The most tangible and visible effect of this program on economic minorities has been to facilitate the higher education of some of its most talented members.

Economic minorities have increasingly found a source of funds available for this purpose in the NDE program. However, this latter contribution should not be exaggerated, for many members of this group cannot take advantage of it since standards of admission to institutions of higher education have not changed to any appreciable extent. (Lately many institutions of higher education have been trying to make some room for members of economic minorities by adjusting admission standards under certain conditions.) The greatest amount of assistance for economic minorities in the area of higher education has come from the opening of new opportunities for them in expanding state colleges coupled with some other forms of state financial aid. While it is true that this greater access to state colleges has been greatly supported by the availability of NDE funds, considerable credit should still go to state governments for any progress in this area.

Finally, the NDE program has contributed to advance the cause of economic minorities by providing special incentives to college graduates who are willing to serve economically disadvantaged groups. In general, it seems safe to suggest that the trend in carrying out the provisions of the act has been toward giving relatively greater consideration to economic minorities, particularly in conjunction with other programs.

The year 1964 witnessed the major legislative effort in the manpower development field on behalf of economic minorities, with the passage of the Economic Opportunity Act (EOA). In its evolution, the EO program has established a family of programs with additional ramifications and working relations with some of the other major programs in the manpower development field.[c]

The primary target of the EO program has been the labor market rehabilitation of the hard to employ members of economic minorities. It has established the Neighborhood Youth Corp and the Job Corps. It has also inaugurated programs such as Work Experience and Training, Operation Mainstream, Special Impact, New Careers and Service, Employment, Redevelopment (Operation SER). It has also established educational programs as part of the overall manpower development effort. Major emphasis has been placed on finding ways to reach out for and motivate economic minorities, particularly those who live at the fringes of society. (In their innovative drive the previously mentioned E&D programs under the MDTA have proved of value). As a complementary task they have tried to generate jobs for them either by creating new types of jobs or by modifying existing ones, particularly by getting employers to change their job contents and/or admission standard whenever this has seemed feasible.

This emphasis of generating new jobs and the like might seem surprising and

[c]This family of programs has been in a constant state of flux. Only the highlights of this family can be discussed here.

could even be construed as a lack of confidence in the ability of manpower development programs to rehabilitate economic minorities completely. But, it is in part explainable by a lack of sufficient funds to provide rehabilitation in depth, even if it were known how to achieve that goal. For example, even after some progress, Congress appropriated only $1.9 billion in 1969 for the entire program. This included funds for supporting services and income allowances, therefore the financing of the direct manpower effort was much less than this figure suggests.[5] Moreover, there is considerable pressure to show quick and substantial results in order to obtain additional funds, since there seems to be some misunderstanding on the part of Congress as to what is involved in the labor market rehabilitation of economic minorities, especially the most deprived.

Finally, the numerous market imperfections that exist tend to limit considerably the number of alternative ways to aid economic minorities. It is impractical to wait until these market imperfections are removed; after all, they might never be. Manpower development has had to be content with simply offsetting them and, it is difficult to do this without risking the introduction of new imperfections. However, it is also conceivable that the sponsors and administrators of such programs lack an adequate understanding of the potentiality of working through the market mechanism. In this respect, in establishing a manpower development strategy in the United States, it has been necessary to train personnel at the same time as the programs were getting under way. This is, of course, a definite short-run handicap in the development of the EO programs that must be taken into account when passing judgment. In general, there has been a sense of urgency, but a lack of direction.

The Community Action Program (CAP) serves as the coordinating arm of the family of programs in the EO set up in order to help deliver the services it can provide to the poor and the disadvantaged. An all out effort has been made, at least in principle, to involve as many interested and influential groups as possible at the local or regional level in the running and development of the program, so as to improve its chances of success. Political appointees, elected officials, representatives of various types of agencies and groups with local interests and, above all, the poor themselves are expected to participate in the establishment of Community Action Agencies (CAA). This permits, in principle, the involvement of the poor, but also of those who can do most to incorporate economic minorities (particularly those with a specific cultural base) into the mainstream of American life, starting at the local level. This was expected to ease group tensions. It was expected that each locality or region could best identify its own problems and try to give to them its own chosen solutions, which hopefully would insure greater support. It was reasoned that different localities may have different problems or at least problems which differ in relative importance. This approach could also serve to channel resources into a common pool, so that the impact would be of the greatest.

One of the EO sub-programs was expected to provide indigenous personnel so that the task of bringing the services that the EO program could in principle provide could be taken directly to the poor with a maximum of efficiency—at least during the early stages when confidence had to be built. It is difficult to discuss the performance of the CAA as a group, for it has considerable freedom concerning organization; nothing close to a pattern has emerged so far, and approximately 1,000 of them are currently in operation.

The establishment of the CAP and CAA by the EO program has raised a very interesting issue which has not been settled, and probably will not be in the near future, short of a major change in legislation. There was considerable disagreement from the beginning as to how much power should be given to the poor in running the program. There is a fine, but important, line between participation and power. On the one hand, the idea of giving as much power to the poor as possible sounded impressive, and some even argued that it would really go a long way toward solving the problems of the poor in America. On the other hand, in many instances, the very state of deprivation in which many of them have lived, sometimes for several generations, renders them rather ineffective in dealing with the broader world. If a realistic approach is to be taken, it is crucial that the larger community, of which they are part, be willing to participate, for this is the only way to shorten the transition period. This participation by the larger group is not likely to come unless it is accompanied by decision-making power. This suggests the need to devote considerable research to determine the maximum participation feasible within a realistic framework.

In servicing the economically and socially disadvantaged, the EO program tries to cater to the many and varied needs of this group, including the different needs of rural and urban residents, thereby spreading thinly its limited resources. While this does have the advantage of extending help to as many groups as possible within the economic minority family, it also means that there is relatively less aid available to each group. However, in this experimental stage this may be a sound approach, particularly to the extent that the laying down of the foundation for a comprehensive attack on the problem is desired. Some programs, such as the Work Experience and Training, include an income maintenance feature with vocational education and work experience to help recipients become more competitive in the labor market. This program has gradually evolved into WIN whose primary target is welfare recipients.

Other aspects of the EO program, such as Operation Mainstream, try to aid older workers in urban and rural areas through what looks like a work program, but actually is just a form of income maintenance. These are usually people who cannot be assigned to existing retraining programs and who are prevented from finding jobs because of age and lack of employment opportunities. (Note how the idea of work in return for assistance is evident in this kind of program.)

Another program, New Careers, tries to develop sub-professional employment for economic minorities by creating jobs connected with existing manpower development programs. This program has grown into the recently created Public Service Careers Program (PSCP) which is expected to help insure that disadvantaged people can find employment, particularly if they have been subject to some training under one of the existing programs. Generating jobs for these people in the public employment sector is one of its primary objectives and makes this program the counterpart of JOBS in the private sector.

Since expansion of the government sector is anticipated to provide one of the major sources of job expansion in the near future, considerable hope is being placed on it, particularly since the government may have more flexibility in employing people since they are under less pressure. Not necessarily having to show profits (or its equivalent), it can manipulate production functions to a greater extent. This is a clear reflection on the existing pressures to make the recipients of any aid perform some work, and on the philosophy permeating the EO program whereby those involved want to see tangible results, which usually mean jobs. This is true under the present institutional structure, but it does not have to be.

The program has been divided into four sub-programs, with a fifth one recently added, so that as many different cases as possible can be handled through them. They are: a) employment and upgrading in state and local governments (the hire now, train later approach); b) employment and upgrading in federal grants-in-aid programs; c) New Careers in human services (where most of the original New Careers program has been absorbed); d) entry employment and upgrading in the federal service. A struggle is in progress to get the Civil Service Commissions to adjust their entry requirements, etc.

The fifth and latest component, Step, tried to meet a problem which has recently arisen, though it was not unexpected—at least not by those familiar with the working of the American economy. It tries to meet the challenge posed by the recession, coupled with insufficient application of the idea of the total social and economic rehabilitation that is necessary in helping many members of the economic minority family. It attempts to find jobs in public-type employment for those who have completed some form of retraining, but cannot find jobs and are not eligible for unemployment insurance. Step provides a clear example of the tremendous learning experience that these experiments in manpower development have brought about, and has exhibited the many problems that exist in assisting this group of people. Above all, it is an attempt to fill in the gap left by the lack of some form of minimum guaranteed income which can throw some of these newly trained people back into abject poverty.

The future of the PSP program is likely to be influenced by the passage of the new Intergovernmental Personnel Act which authorizes assistance of various kinds to help improve the quality of public service and the employment of handicapped and disadvantaged people. This program may play an important role in developing the foundations of a form of guaranteed job scheme of a short-term, as well as a long-term character. Because of the state of flux of these programs, it should not be surprising, however, that when the recession is over, this aspect of the EO program is deemphasized.

But, the major effort of the EO family of programs has been geared to help young people by encouraging and assisting them to stay in school, or by aiding them to gain work experience while receiving some income, for example the Job Corps which, in some instances, has established non-residential centers in both rural and urban areas intended to equip young people to enter the labor market by providing them with education, training and work experience, simultaneously. These centers are conceptually similar to the MDT skill centers. If the latter continue to place relatively more emphasis on economic minorities, this might lead to overlapping. But, given the present institutional setup, the centers should be available, for disadvantaged members of economic minorities may need special supportive services and sometimes different methods of learning than other groups.

In addition to the Job Corps, there is the Neighborhood Youth Corps component to assist young people to stay in and/or return to school while earning some income by working part-time or during the summers. It also has an out-of-school program to assist young people, school dropouts for the most part, to gain some supervised work experience while receiving some financial assistance, too. To some extent the provisions of the 1967 Amendment to the Social Security Act have encouraged young people from welfare families to work while staying in school, for their income from work is now not subject to any loss in welfare payments, and even those not in school are subject to some income exemption.

That young people have been at the top of the priority list is suggested by budget allocations within the EO family. For example, the Neighborhood Youth Corps has been receiving the largest share of all programs. (This is excluding the assistance provided through the strictly educational component of the EO family of programs.)

Finally, and most important of all, the family of EO programs has attempted to take into consideration the fact that the employment rehabilitation of economic minorities requires, in many instances, a battery of supportive services, including legal services, health care, transportation, and babysitting.[6] This has been provided not only through some of the individual programs but also through the Neighborhood Centers already referred to. This suggests a growing realization that in aiding economic minorities, the need for social and economic rehabilitation is central.

The EO program has been experimenting with a new concept in manpower development for economic minorities, namely the Concentrated Employment Program (CEP). It has been designed to combine manpower development services and the other supportive services necessary to help an individual move from a condition of unemployability and dependency to one of self-sufficiency. The novelty consists in delivering all these services through one single source. Formerly, these various services were being offered under separate programs, sometimes programs even outside the EO structure. Professor Garth L. Mangum has commented that conceptually, CEP could provide a mechanism for integrating fragmented federal programs—as have been seen to exist—into useful combinations of services tailored to meet local needs.[7]

As things stand now there are many overlapping sub-programs resulting in much confusion. Moreover, a more nearly optimal utilization of the very limited amount of expertise available in this area is essential, at least until a more adequate supply might become available. The above should not be construed as a major criticism as far as the 1960s are concerned; this was a decade of experimentation, with everyone trying to develop and test new ways to cope with the problems afflicting economic minorities. The decade of the 1970s, however, must be one of consolidation and progress, for economic minorities cannot wait forever. Further exploration of new means to attain the ultimate goal is still needed, but should be simultaneous with further progress in regard to experience so far achieved.

The existence of two other aspects of the War on Poverty, as the EO program has come to be known, should at least be mentioned. The first is the purely educational aspect, of major significance in the development of our human resource base. This includes the Head Start program whose central concern is to equip the children of economic minorities so that they can make their entry into the school system with a minimum of disadvantage. Through this program, a variety of supportive services are also provided to insure that no future handicaps, like poor health, may reduce the overall effectiveness of the effort against poverty. It tries, in principle, to tackle the poverty problem in the earliest possible years. It represents a very important part of the foundation which needs to be laid down for the long-run rehabilitation of economic minorities. The second program is Upward Bound which assists members of economic minorities to enter college by providing them with academic and financial assistance. This program was recently combined with Talent Search.

The second aspect is intended to focus attention on some special groups within the economic minority family. One program in this area is SER, primarily designed to assist disadvantaged Spanish-American groups in areas where such groups are large. It seems appropriate to add here that there is also a program for Indians on federal reservations who are disadvantaged.

This author is of the opinion that the point has already been reached in the development of the EO program where Congress should define much more clearly the role and objectives of the program. At this point it is hard to say what is intended: to provide some form of guaranteed job, or guaranteed income, or to serve as an instrument for the economic and social rehabilitation of economic minorities.

If the EO program is here to stay, this author would much prefer that its activities be confined to the manpower development field, including supportive services if necessary, and that it not get involved in any guaranteed job and/or income scheme. Forms of economic security strategy other than manpower development are better provided on a national basis as part of an overall economic security strategy with equal access for everyone. This would mean that if EO participants could not find a job at a later point, or if their incomes were temporarily inadequate they could always have recourse to these other programs. The greatest difficulty at this critical point is the hesitant attitude of Congress, which forces programs like EO to attempt to do things they might not be equipped to do, thus diverting resources away from direct manpower objectives.

Perhaps the program that has done most to demonstrate what manpower development can do for an individual when resources are relatively abundant is the Vocational Rehabilitation program administered by the Rehabilitation

Services Administration. This program is concerned with the rehabilitation of the physically handicapped, and has been equipped to deliver many of the supportive services that people may need during their economic and social rehabilitation. In addition, a very thorough evaluation of the candidate's potential is undertaken in order to reduce the chances of failure. This facilitates the best possible utilization of available resources as well as greater consideration of the needs of the clients. It is relatively the best endowed of all the programs related to manpower development in the United States.

An interesting and provocative point that has been raised is that by stretching the meaning of the term 'handicapped' to include other than physically handicapped, the program could serve many members of economic minorities, for they are in one way or another handicapped when it comes to taking their place in society, particularly those that have been members of the economic minority family for several generations. In some instances because of poor health, poor nutrition, etc., they are very close to being physically handicapped.

A few observations on the 1967 Amendment to the Social Security Act would appear to be relevant at this point. First, since it appears that job training under this act is to be provided through existing manpower development programs, it is not at all clear to what extent long-term rehabilitation is envisaged in its job training feature, so it is difficult to see how this program intends to improve the relative position of economic minorities, except to the extent that manpower programs are independently improved, for this might prove a windfall gain to people in this program since there is provision for them to be referred to such programs. One positive side of the act is, however, that people who receive welfare have been given some incentive to earn income from work since it will not result in a complete loss of welfare assistance, but this does not solve the fundamental problem of labor market rehabilitation. Moreover, since in many states, unemployed people are still not entitled to welfare assistance, even if not receiving unemployment compensation, it does not appear that this work incentive has any major significance, at least not thus far.

Second, the program has its own built-in guaranteed income system, but in the form of a welfare-guaranteed job combination, which suggests that it is more concerned with justifying the payment of an income than it is with the whole idea of rehabilitation.

Finally, the act's interest in the establishment of day care centers for potential working mothers, if and when it becomes a reality, would have a definite impact upon the labor force. Inasmuch as participation of would-be working mothers is voluntary, the program may prove of value in the war against poverty. However, if training and employment is forced upon economic minorities the whole idea may be highly questionable and fundamentally at odds with values held by many people in this society. This is an issue with many social ramifications and deserves to be examined as part of a broader framework, a task not to be undertaken here.

There is one institution which has undergone considerable change in an effort to assist this nation in the development of a manpower development strategy:

the U.S. Public Employment Service which was originally created in the 1930s. As originally conceived, it was supposed to be a job exchange but it has gradually evolved, particularly during the 1960s, into more of a manpower agency. This transformation has been greatly aided by the increased tendency to separate the unemployment insurance mechanism from the purely employment standpoint.

In its new role, the service geared its effort at first to manpower training problems, particularly by referring people for retraining. But, its role has also included analysis of labor market conditions, and, with the passage of the EOA, the service has increasingly become involved with the plight of economic minorities to deal with which it has made a special effort to train personnel and the like. In its bid to help economic minorities, the service has established working connections with the major existing manpower development programs including CAA through which most of the work on behalf of economic minorities has to be channeled. This is particularly important since both the Employment Service and CAA are both organized on a local-regional basis. The service's new image has proved particularly useful in developing the team approach to increase the employability of disadvantaged people whereby all kinds of services are provided through a team effort.

The development of an early warning system where mass layoffs are anticipated is also being developed. It may prove very useful in averting the occurrence of pockets of unemployment resulting from such actions which, in turn, may degenerate into pockets of poverty. The Employment Service can provide both employers and workers with information on all available services to assist them in adjusting to the change and can then assist them to obtain such services.

Another aspect that has received considerable attention is the development of a job bank, so that the clearing mechanism of the Employment Service can be improved. This job exchange role has important implications for manpower development because it increases the amount of information on jobs and personnel available, a factor that tends to make markets more effective.

During 1970, an experimental "Three-Tiered Employment Office" with the idea of developing the Employment Service into a Comprehensive Manpower Agency was set in motion on a small scale. The three levels of services offered are: a) a streamlined, self-help service; b) a combination of job development and direction in planning a personal job search; c) an intensive employability service to the most disadvantaged, which is expected to include reliance on the job bank mechanism already referred to. The central idea is to take into account the manpower needs of different clients.

In principle, it should not be difficult for the Employment Service to become the main coordinator of this nation's manpower development strategy, since it is in an excellent position, if properly equipped, to know the direction in which programs should move. This is particularly true if manpower development strategies are kept separate from other economic security strategies. In this connection, the Employment Service has already been affected in one way or another by most of the manpower development connected legislation passed during the 1960s. The Employment Service is another example of a manpower related agency that has gradually shifted its emphasis to aid economic minorities, particularly by taking an active role and reaching out to where the need is, rather than waiting for things to happen.

The above list does not exhaust all the existing manpower programs, but it does include most of the important ones. Other legislation with manpower development overtones includes: the Health Professions Educational Act of 1963, the Nurse Training Act of 1964, the Allied Health Professions Personnel Act of 1966 and the Health Manpower Act of 1968. This group shows the mounting pressures that exist to improve our national health programs—a very important factor in any attempt to assist economic minorities—and also to provide some economic security for many of those who are not members of the economic minority population. It is a specific effort to influence a certain sector of the economy. Although, in general, this can be viewed as going against the philosophy underlying this work (reliance on the market would be greatly preferred) it can also be viewed as the only presently realistic way to deal with a problem where the solution has long been overdue, mostly as a result of market imperfections.

The Higher Education Act of 1965 should be included in this summary too, for it has important implications for manpower development in general, and economic minorities in particular. Of special significance is its development of the work-study program which was originally authorized by the EOA. This program has played an important role in assisting low income students to earn income from work while attending college. The act also established the Teacher Corps to provide teaching manpower in areas with a high concentration of children from low income families. In 1968 another educational-related act was passed—the Adult Basic Education Act. Its main purpose was to help adults who were finding it increasingly difficult to compete in the job market when unemployed, because of serious deficiencies in basic skills.

The year 1965 also witnessed the enactment of the Public Works and Economic Development Act which was intended to replace the Area Redevelopment Act of 1961, particularly the non-manpower development aspect of the act, since the manpower related ones were absorbed largely by the MDT program.

That year also saw the Appalachian Aid Bill passed. This bill is, in principle, similar to the Economic Development Act. The Civil Rights Act of 1964 ought to be included here, too, for it occupies a very special place in any attempt to develop a manpower development strategy. It was intended to eliminate one of the greatest and least justifiable of man-made market imperfections—racial discrimination. Manpower development programs are likely to be much less effective in the absence of a legal framework that encourages equality of opportunity.

Finally, the American armed forces have been a major source of training and education, either directly or indirectly, through the GI Bill. It has recently become very important in providing financial assistance to GIs with relatively low educational achievement to help them make the adjustment to the civilian labor force. This program has been greatly supplemented by the Veteran's Readjustment Benefits Act of 1966. All these sources of manpower development mentioned above have one thing in common: they all have contributed, in differing degrees and sometimes only indirectly, in advancing the cause of economic minorities in this country.

It is beyond the scope of this study to discuss manpower development policies for economic minorities at the state and local levels, but such programs do exist, though their value varies tremendously from one place to another. For the most part, their major contribution has come through cooperation with federal agencies, by invoking the mechanism of grants-in-aid, or using state and/or local initiative to obtain funds to organize manpower development programs. That substantial state and local participation exists was demonstrated by the use of the CAA mechanism in developing the EO setup, and by the increased reliance on the Public Employment Service structure. This approach is very much in line with the political organization of this country, and tends to encourage grass roots support and participation. However, if and when state and/or local governments fail to discharge their responsibility in the manpower development field and in the battle against poverty, there would seem to be no other alternative than for the federal government to set into motion its own machinery.

Finally, the business sector is making a greater effort to employ members of economic minorities. This effort is being channeled through the National Alliance of Businessmen (NAB) and the Job Opportunities in the Business Sector Program (JOBS). It is basically an OJT approach, though in assisting disadvantaged workers, some supportive services have been provided. This is, in part, what has raised the cost per trainee, as explained earlier in this section. The major thrust of the program has been in metropolitan areas, although the Labor Department has been authorized to engage in contracting in any part of the country. The Administration has been trying to promote this program, and its goal was to have close to 650,000 enrollees by 1971 (between 1968 and 1970 some 560,000 individuals were hired), but the latest recession has been a big stumbling block.[d]

This effort by the business sector, though perhaps morally commendable, is economically misguided. In the first place, as soon as the economy starts to recede work is likely to collapse, if only partially; or if continued, would have to be done at the expense of non-economic minority workers which would be likely to alienate the general public. It should be borne in mind that most of these trainees are hired for production-type jobs which are the most affected by changes in the level of economic activity.

Second, this effort is for the most part not carried out at company's expense, but is subsidized by federal and/or state governments. If what is needed is just the equipment and instructors to train people, then this could be arranged

---

[d]It has been reported that employers have sometimes hired disadvantaged workers on their own without asking for the subsidy.

differently. The problem is that most of this training is specific in nature rather than general, thus having limited transferability to other jobs. A better contribution to solving the problems of economic minorities would be made by simply putting an end to discriminatory and unrealistic hiring practices wherever they exist.

Last, but by no means least, the major responsibility of the business sector to this nation consists in being as efficient as possible and not in attempting to do social work which, in the final analysis will have to be paid for by consumers in general. This sector can certainly make a very significant contribution to the economy of this country by operating efficiently while respecting the rules of free market economics, for example by ending monopolistic practices which, in many instances, are conducive to lower levels of employment through output restrictions, not to mention a distorted income distribution.

In conclusion, it seems clear that at least in principle, legislative intent has increasingly moved toward providing greater assistance to economic minorities. This seems to have occurred even in programs where the plight of economic minorities was not originally the major target. Faced with the impact of a recession, Congress has shown a rather hesitant attitude. There seems to have been a tendency to de-emphasize temporarily the rehabilitation aspect of the problem in order to give greater assistance to other groups with a stronger political base.

This author is not unqualifiedly critical of giving aid to the latter, but he is very critical of any attempt to do so at the expense of current efforts on behalf of economic minorities. This problem will be greatly reduced once this country has established more effective means of protecting the nation as a whole against the threat of economic insecurity. This ought to be done concurrently with any special effort to aid economic minorities, for it is part and parcel of the same problem. However, a salient point is the fact that Congress did not rush to scrap programs in the face of a crisis, but rather tried to use the manpower development mechanism to help a number of different groups. This suggests that the seeds for the development of a more comprehensive and permanent manpower development strategy may have been planted. This is a very significant forward step even if at this point the shape of such a program is not entirely clear, particularly because experimentation has been going on in so many different, sometimes conflicting, directions.

Thus far, Congress has not been generous enough with manpower development programs designed to aid economic minorities, though its appropriations for manpower development and supportive programs in general have been growing. For example, by 1969 the federal government alone was spending over $2 billion a year in manpower development programs. But, as discussed, earlier, by no means all of this goes to economic minorities. Total federal assistance to the poor on all accounts was approximately $25 billion in 1960 and is expected to rise to nearly $31 billion by 1971. However, the EO program—the major program for economic minorities—is receiving a little under $2 billion and it should be remembered that it represents a combination of income supplements, training program, and general rehabilitation.

The experimental nature of the decade of the 1960s might partially account for Congress' preference for trying many ideas on a small scale; being conservative would probably elicit greater public support in the long-run. On the other hand, Congress has to learn to be somewhat more patient with problems where the solutions are long-term in nature, like the employment rehabilitation of economic minorities.

If this country is demanding patience on the part of economic minorities, Congress and constituents alike will have to reciprocate, particularly if good faith is to be established during this very painful period of transition. Congress should, of course, keep a close surveillance over how the various programs are being run, but in a more realistic fashion.

7

Summary and Outlook for the 1970s

In this first part, major changes that have been—and promise to continue—taking place in the American economy for the past two decades and which have brought about a profound transformation in its structure were examined. It was seen how such changes are increasingly demanding new means of coping with the kinds of economic insecurity that seem to follow in the wake. A case was made for the exploration and development of such means and ways that would strengthen rather than weaken the performance of the market system on which the American economy is supposed to rest (though at times this appears to be forgotten).

Particular emphasis was placed on showing how manpower development is central to the idea of providing economic security within the existing framework and how it is possible to develop a policy along these lines which does not conflict with the basic tenets of the market system, but is, in fact, essential to its viability. It was explained that no exception to this has to be made in tackling the particular case of economic minorities. It was also explained that manpower development should be the foundation on which to build such a system of economic defense, supplemented by an adequate combined social security guaranteed minimum income structure.

The manpower development and income provision revolution that has been taking place over the past decade was thoroughly examined and it was noted that, increasingly, the plight of economic minorities has been taken into account by this legislation, although at times in a rather inadequate fashion. Of particular interest is the fact that even in times of crisis, the programs have been maintained, although admittedly in a rather haphazard and controversial fashion. What remains to be discussed briefly here are the implications of all these developments for the current decade.

Progress is very seldom unaccompanied by new problems, and the progress brought about by the manpower development revolution and new attitudes towards the issue of economic security in general are no exception to this. As new programs have been established and experimented with, new problems have surfaced; yet a feeling of what it is possible to accomplish, a degree of hopefulness, seem to have emerged, and the foundations on which to build a better strategy seem to have been gradually and painfully erected.

As this country enters the decade of the 1970s, it is confronted with a group of rather ill-coordinated efforts, each one showing only partial results. This then is the time to inaugurate a new and revitalized effort to conquer the malady of economic insecurity without abandoning our system of values, but modernizing

87

them to meet the new challenge. Already under way are some attempts to consolidate or, at least to coordinate, efforts.

The streamlining of the U.S. Employment Service and the CEP are two examples. Attempts to separate the training from the purely educational aspects of manpower development and to separate both from programs trying just to provide some form of income are also illustrations of this gradual, but steady, development in this direction.

The major stumbling block at this point is the apparent inability to decide whether guaranteed jobs or guaranteed minimum incomes should be at the center of the provision of a minimum of economic security in the current decade. As explained earlier, each has different manpower development implications. The recession that has been afflicting the American economy has been a definite drawback, because Congress as well as the Administration, have been under fire to alleviate the short-run problems posed by the recession. However, a greater realization has evolved from this experience: manpower development can be of great value in reducing the impact of recessions. The fact that attempts have been made to work through it attests to this.

A movement toward decentralization has been at the heart of both the 1969 proposed Manpower Act and the newly proposed Manpower Revenue Sharing Act of 1971. The central idea is to provide a single flexible grant to states (and certain local governments that qualify) rather than many separate grants-in-aid. This is a significant step toward a comprehensive attack on the problem but it is still too early to know how the states will respond in practice. In the Manpower Revenue Sharing Act of 1971, 85 percent of funds so allocated are expected to go for training and employment activities; the other 15 percent for activities carried out by the Secretary of Labor which includes technical assistance of various kinds to states and the establishment of a national computerized job bank program. Both acts have recommended a built-in mechanism to release funds for encouraging training and assistance whenever the rate of unemployment equals or exceeds 4.5 percent for 3 consecutive months. They also provide for the repeal of the MDTA and the EOA. This, together with the gradual conversion of the U.S. Employment Service into a Comprehensive Manpower Agency System would become the base of this nation's manpower development strategy during the current decade. Greater cooperation would be needed, however, with the American educational system to secure the greatest possible effect. Particularly greater cooperation with the system of vocational education would be necessary.

These recommendations tend to fit rather well, in principle, with the previous work of CAA whereby each region was encouraged to identify its own needs and try to establish programs satisfactory to people living in the area and, of course, effective in solving their problem. The idea of setting up a separate corporation to deal with all manpower development-related problems has been advanced in some quarters. Further exploration of this idea should not be abandoned.

One of the major problems that this Administration still is not facing squarely is the need for much larger budget appropriations to back up its manpower development effort. Approximately $2 billion for manpower development is being requested. This is too low a figure in any program in which the in-depth social and economic rehabilitation of economic minorities has top priority. It might have been a workable figure in the 1960s—due to the experimental nature of the programs—but not in the current decade.

On the other front, the President's proposal for the provision of a guaranteed minimum income of $2,400 for a family of four (including the food stamp program) is very much alive. So, the idea of a guaranteed minimum income has not been abandoned, except that it does not cover everyone who might need this assistance and that it carries very stringent work requirements for potential recipients—stringent considering that retraining programs are just beginning to recognize the true meaning of social and economic rehabilitation in assisting many of these people.

It seems apparent that the above figure is inadequate by now and that the system should have a built-in mechanism to insure that the minimum level of assistance is periodically revised to reflect changes in the level of affluence of this nation. If the automatic trigger of the newly proposed manpower Act does work, many of the unemployed will probably wind up doing some work for the government, if only on a temporary basis. In a sense what is evolving is a hybrid, though it is likely that by the end of the decade one of the two (guaranteed jobs or guaranteed minimum income) will emerge victorious, particularly if manpower development policies become more effective, because fewer people would need income supplements. There seems to be no intention to scrap the Social Insurance Mechanism, and the more its structure is improved, the less would be the need to resort to the guaranteed income mechanism.

It is quite possible that some further consolidation of these different strategies will be achieved during the 1970s and that as the next decade approaches, manpower development will be at the very base of the nation's economic security strategy, as it should be. However, it is still too early to say.

The establishment of this new foundation means that this country will be able to advance on the economic front with less fear. Such confidence is of paramount importance if progress is to be encouraged, particularly since it is almost certain to be based on technological changes where impact on the labor force is still very much of a mystery.

In closing, it is important to indicate that some of these policies may, at times, work against the basic principle underlying this study, i.e., that the performance of the market economy be improved by their actions. Most of the policies instituted during the 1960s were not in basic conflict with this principle, though the way they were administered might have been. To the extent that they were dictated by expediency, such aberrations might be justified in part, but in this newly developing manpower-guaranteed income platform, such expediency would be intolerable.

To the extent that lack of knowledge as to how to proceed was the excuse, it would be an unacceptable excuse in this new decade of progress in this field.

Finally, to the extent that these policies or their implementation represented

iberate attempt to manipulate the market mechanism, they are open to
ıs questioning. The 1970s should prove valuable in indicating in what
direction we are really moving in the above regard.

This nation has come a long way in developing adequate means to provide a
minimum of economic security and in putting substance and meaning into the
empty shell of the 1946 Employment Act. It is important to realize that this
transformation has been a very gradual one, over a period of almost four
decades. However, there is still a long way to go, and a slowing down of this
effort now is the last thing this country can afford.

**Part II:
Labor Mobility and
Resettlement Programs in
Manpower Development**

8 Labor Mobility and the Market Mechanism: An Introduction

This portion of the study will focus on one particular form of manpower development—labor mobility—and the contribution that this type of manpower development can make towards the rehabilitation of economic minorities. It is relevant to examine first the importance of labor mobility to the market mechanism, with particular reference to migration, as well as the extent of voluntary migration in the United States.

The smooth operation of a dynamic market economy calls for a great deal of factor mobility, because its equilibrium is in a constant state of flux. This suggests that anything which impedes factor mobility ought to be removed. It is important to realize, however, that factor mobility *per se* is no guarantee that the efficiency of the market mechanism in allocating scarce economic resources will improve. Indeed, it could even be perverse if workers and producers misread market signals. This may occur when inadequate information and other market imperfections, like housing discrimination, exist. Not only could it be perverse but it could also be the source of new disequilibrium, particularly if more factor mobility than is actually necessary takes place. It is important to bear in mind that in order to bring about adjustment, it is sufficient that only some factors of production move.

In principle, a flexible wage structure, in the case of labor, would tend to redistribute labor to adjust to changes in the economy. Wage flexibility is the traditional neoclassical recipe. There seems to be sufficient evidence that the wage structure does tend to change.[a] The reason some people think it does not adjust is that they are usually looking at the basic wage rate instead of actual earnings from work. However, it may not adjust within what is socially acceptable as a reasonable period of time due to market imperfections and institutional factors that tend to retard such adjustment. It is possible that these drawbacks might have become more acute in the course of time. To the extent that the number and seriousness of these imperfections has been growing, it is, for the most part, less possible to rely on such a mechanism. There is, for example, some recent evidence that voluntary labor mobility may have been decreasing, which hints at the above possibility, a problem that may have been aggravated by the structure of unemployment permeating the American economy over the past 10 or 15 years.[1]

With regard to labor mobility, it is a fact that it is far from perfect. This is particularly true of geographical mobility, the type of mobility of principal interest to this study. It has to be recognized that geographical mobility usually

[a]There is a very large literature on wage structure supporting this view.

encompasses occupational and/or industrial mobility, too, which makes the move a more difficult challenge. Besides, it presents special sociological problems related to the emotional adjustment involved which may be difficult to measure in assessing the degree of responsiveness of the labor force in this respect. It is conceivable that once this sort of factor is taken into account the degree of responsiveness of the labor force may be greater than it seems.

Concerning the occupational changes that are usually necessary when migration occurs, 'major' occupational mobility seems to pose a very special challenge. Because of the complexity involved in a major occupational change, it may be difficult to achieve within a single generation. (Of course, non-major occupational changes are possible within shorter periods of time, as past experience suggests.) As more of these major occupational changes are needed, voluntary migration may be adversely affected, since workers may come to think that moving to another region would not in itself improve their chances of finding jobs.

Labor mobility is not the only adjustment mechanism which exists. While these major occupational changes are slowly taking place, particularly through attrition and new entries, there is the possibility of resorting to capital-labor substitution. This may be accompanied by technological adjustments, too. The latter is important, for in the process of substituting capital for labor, it is sometimes feasible to substitute one type of labor for another. This may facilitate migration, because it reduces the need to undergo a major occupational change that is beyond the reach of many workers, at least within a relatively short period of time. Also, capital may be discouraged from moving in, to the extent that wages are maintained relatively high (given changes in demand and supply conditions) either artificially or because of resistance to accepting lower wages in a region where labor is in relatively ample supply.

Another important adjustment mechanism which is usually though of as in competition with labor mobility, although it does not have to be, is locational adjustment—that is, production can be moved to where costs turn out to be least (after changes in the structure of the economy). It can be complementary to labor mobility for it might also result in in-migration of some labor to those areas.

From a policy point of view, it is always possible to have recourse to still another major adjustment mechanism, namely regional development. This is usually undertaken to make the region relatively more attractive for production, thus it is not entirely independent of the above adjustment mechanisms, particularly the locational one. That this policy has been used in the United States was seen in the preceding section when the passage of some acts whose primary intention was regional development was mentioned.

Indeed, all these adjustment mechanisms can be set in motion simultaneously to make the task easier, for they are not mutually exclusive processes, especially when the relative price structure is rather inflexible so that it cannot be relied on heavily to do the job. However, there is usually a tendency, for one adjustment mechanism to be relatively more important depending upon the particular circumstances surrounding the change in question. For example, the migration of capital to a region can increase the demand for labor, assuming that local labor can be employed. In addition to the employment of more people, it can also increase the capital labor ratio which, in turn, increases the productivity of labor. This process can be further encouraged by adequate development of the region so as to attract production to it.

A responsive labor force, however, would simply make the whole process a lot easier. Besides, there may be times when other adjustment mechanisms might not be able to work due to market imperfections or the institutional framework in which these various adjustment mechanisms have to function. But above all, in an economy where heavy reliance is placed on labor mobility to facilitate change, migration becomes a very important factor, and the efficient operation of that market could be greatly strengthened by helping to maintain a labor force responsive to change and capable of interpreting adequately market signals.

An illustration of why the above is so important and why reliance on other mechanisms may not always be feasible is given by capital and labor not moving in opposite directions, but in the same one. In a recent study, supporting evidence was found for the view that capital and labor seem to have been moving in the same direction.[2] This pattern seems to have been the result of capital and labor migration being largely responsive to expected future earnings and not necessarily to the existing structure of relative prices, particularly the wage structure, except to the extent that future rates of return to factors of production are influenced by current ones. Of course, it is likely that many people, due to inadequate information and the like, may use the present structure as a reflection of future trends. It is important to bear in mind, however, that this phenomenon may be influenced, if only partially, by the fact that the current structure may not be very flexible, for if it were, it would influence present expectations about future earnings.

This kind of finding, given the present institutional framework, does not seem unrealistic, for it is possible that the same area proves attractive to both capital and labor. This, of course, creates a rather tragic situation for areas losing labor, because they tend to lose their most promising labor, leaving behind older and less educated workers who, in addition, have generally been found to be among the less mobile groups. To the extent that they are successful in defending their average wage level amid the decline in the quality of labor, the result tends to be unemployment and eventually poverty. There is nothing in economic analysis to suggest that some regions will never go economically bankrupt; however, politically, it is usually hard to abandon them. The major problem in trying to implement economic development policies to offset such decline is that this is often attempted once the problem has become critical.

In discussing migration, it is significant to make some mention of the degree of willingness of people to change jobs and occupations. American workers have shown a rather strong willingness to change jobs. One problem has been that given the present institutional framework, quite often this requires quitting one's current job first which sometimes results in having to settle for a less attractive job. A few years ago Professor L. Reynolds showed evidence that a very large percentage of workers who quit a job to search for another one wind up with lower wages.[3] This seems to be especially true among low skilled labor due to the way in which labor markets operate within a firm (internal labor markets) whereby a person is frequently hired at the port of entry of the firm and then works his way up through a rather well established hierarchy of jobs and occupations.

In changing jobs, American labor has also shown a marked inclination to change occupations, if only within the same general level of skill in a given generation. For example, a recent report by the Bureau of Labor Statistics shows that between 1965 and 1966, some 5.5 million people 18 years of age and over changed occupations out of a labor force of 70 million people.[4] Interestingly enough, quite often the change was from blue collar to white collar and service occupations which suggests some degree of lateral mobility. This change in occupation was usually accompanied by a change of industry and employer.

The general pattern in the above respect was found similar to that existing after World War II. This suggests that willingness to move regionally is not greatly hindered by the likely need to change occupations and/or industries, at least not to a significant extent yet. This might suggest that other adjustment mechanisms may have been lessening the need to make major occupational changes within the same generation.

The U.S. Department of Commerce has reported that while in any given year, only about 5 percent of the population are mobile, (they move between labor markets), over their lifetime, most people tend to move out of the area where they are born.[5] For example, only approximately 30 percent of family heads in 1960 were born in the same area where they were living. Another illustration of people's willingness to move is given by the fact that some 16 percent of heads of household in 1960 moved to where they were then living within the previous 5 years, and only 27 percent of those who had been in the same area since 1950 were born there and never lived elsewhere.[6] This evidence, while not proving that migration has been effective in improving the performance of labor markets, does suggest the relatively high willingness of people to move in response to changing economic conditions.

An important aspect of the analysis of voluntary migration is the extent to which unemployed workers show a relatively higher propensity to migrate than employed workers. Relatively higher rates of migration among unemployed workers is, on the average, a healthy sign, especially if their unemployment is of a structural type. In general, the available evidence is somewhat conflicting.

There is some evidence that, at least during the 1950s, unemployed workers did seem to exhibit relatively higher rates of migration.[7] However, some more recent evidence suggests both groups have shown about the same rate of migration, or at least that unemployment *per se* was not a significant driving force.[8]

The following factors may help to account for this situation. In the first place, it was mentioned before that there is some evidence the willingness to change jobs in general may be declining. This may account, in part, for the relative decline in the willingness to move among unemployed workers. Second, it was noted earlier that during the 1960s quite a few programs to aid in the retraining of workers and the alleviation of poverty in depressed areas were established. It is conceivable that they did have some effect on the willingness of unemployed workers to resort to this adjustment mechanism, namely migration; they may have increased their hopes of finding employment locally. Third, it is possible that among those employed workers who moved, some were anticipating displacement and some were really underemployed who could have been reported as unemployed workers in a sense. Finally, it is possible that structurally unemployed workers may have found it increasingly difficult to move since the jobs open in other regions may not have been available to them due to their skill content.

Some workers may have even left the labor force, as was seen earlier in this study, when confronted with an inability to find any job. Higher central city unemployment rates among low skilled—less educated workers hints at this possibility. It seems that the urban labor market may have had some difficulty in absorbing migrants in this category. It is also important to bear in mind that low-skilled and less educated workers have tended to show lower than average migration rates, and if they have been the groups most affected by changes in the economy, it stands to reason that this will tend to show in the migration rates of unemployed workers.[9]

While these factors may not be sufficient to account for such a phenomenon, they certainly suggest it. Some of these problems are, of course, very relevant in justifying migration policies as part of a national manpower strategy for they point to the existence of deep rooted problems which may be hard to overcome by unassisted market forces within the present institutional framework and which may have grave consequences in an advanced industrial environment, particularly for economic minorities.

In part, because of some of these problems, or because of the lack of means to assist them to move out, or both, there is some evidence that people living in so-called depressed areas are not relatively inclined to migrate as much as people in other areas. Of course, the problem of depressed areas goes beyond the economic ones; there may be some cultural problems affecting their willingness to migrate. Besides, as discussed in Part I, legislation such as the ARA, was intended to discourage people from moving out. The experience so far suggests that area redevelopment still has a lot to prove itself, though it is still too early to properly assess it. Therefore, the migration mechanism still has very much to recommend it.

At the aggregate level, there has been a strong tendency for people to move to regions where wages are, on the average, relatively high and jobs relatively plentiful.[10] This, of course, does not say much about the cross-movement of people, nor does it say much about the extent to which the skills of the migrants match those required in the vacant jobs, that is whether migration contributes to clear the market at prevailing wage rates. However, at least it suggests that, in principle, it has been in the right direction. Also supporting this view is the fact that high unemployment areas have been net losers of population and low unemployment areas net gainers. For example, net migration between 1955 and 1960 as a percentage of the 1960 population in a selected sample shows that the former lost, on the average, 3.2 percent while the former gained, on the average, 3.1 percent. This was accompanied by considerable cross migration which, in principle, is also a healthy sign.[11]

One of the most heated debates in the literature on migration, though recently it has been waning, has been whether job availability or higher wage rates is the dominant force in migration. As suggested above, both seem to be of consequence. The problem is that there seems to be no incompatibility between them, for they represent two aspects of the same market process, namely price and quantity adjustments. They are interconnected to the point that higher wage rates and availability of jobs are likely to come together. However, if sufficient people would respond to the availability of jobs, then wage rates would not have to increase as fast. The usual counterargument to this is: how can we explain the presence of higher wage rates in some labor markets while people are unemployed? Apart from existing imperfections in the market place, labor is not homogeneous and it is possible that unemployed labor cannot be transferred within the same labor market, at least not in the short-run.

The evidence presented here though not conclusive, does strongly support the view that on the average, migration seems to have had a positive effect in facilitating the operation of the market mechanism, if only perhaps in an imperfect fashion. Be that as it may, the fact that American workers are relatively inclined to move when conditions appear propitious suggests that labor mobility programs have a lot to offer, for they can be instituted without major institutional changes.

In closing, it is relevant to discuss the particular situation of economic minorities with regard to their propensity to move. In general, there is no evidence that economic minorities are reluctant to move, though they may face some additional problems. The fact that, on the average, migration rates among people with low incomes are lower than among people with high incomes, at least in the case of people between the ages of 25 and 44 as the evidence in table A-17 shows, is not sufficient evidence that economic minorities are relatively less mobile *per se*. Low incomes are usually associated with below average education and low skills, two factors that tend to be associated with below average rates of migration. This, as will be discussed in the next section, is likely to reflect the investment character of migration since the above two factors may reduce the relative value of migration. Besides, it is likely that many people in the lowest income groups are welfare recipients for whom the present structure of the American welfare system may be serving to hinder migration due, for example, to resident requirements and the like. Table A-17 does show, however, that although the same association between income level and migration exists for non-white groups, the latter do seem to have somewhat lower rates of migration. Nevertheless, the average propensity to migrate of both groups is still rather high.

The heavy outmigration of blacks to the North, and of Puerto Ricans and Mexican American to many cities of the United States, supports the view that these groups are also ready to move when the opportunity for advancement is present. They might be reluctant to move at times, however, particularly for the following two reasons: first, they might fear that economic and social conditions in the new location may prove to be little better than in the old, that their choice is between farm and slum. Second, they might fear to encounter social prejudice. (Later in this study some measures that have been used in experimental mobility programs to overcome this particular sort of barrier are discussed.) The chances are that any perverse migration as might have taken place in the United States may have been relatively greater among economic minorities, not only because lack of adequate knowledge about the market is likely to be greater among economic minorities, but also because, due to discriminatory policies in housing and jobs, they may be forced to migrate where they can rather than to where they might be able to make the greatest contribution.

But, probably the most serious obstacle in their way is that no matter how valuable migration may promise to be, they may not have the means to avail themselves of it. All this suggests the tremendous significance of mobility projects and of measures to improve the labor mobility of this group in general. Not only can they help to reduce poverty, but they can do this while improving the efficiency of the market mechanism.

Labor Mobility Programs in Manpower Development

The objectives of this section are threefold: to discuss the role of labor mobility in manpower development; to explore current efforts in the United States to develop labor mobility programs, and to establish a framework within which to examine the empirical work to be discussed in the next section. This last objective, however, is not independent of the other two, but rather an underlying factor.

Labor mobility can lead to increases in productivity through a better allocation of resources; therefore, it can be a very important manpower development weapon. Take, for example, the case of an unemployed worker in a depressed area while there are job vacancies that he could fill somewhere else. Labor mobility can be seen as another form of investment in human capital of the same nature as skill development or health maintenance. In principle, then, individuals in a market-oriented economy should be free to decide how much they want to spend in this form of investment. If they wish to maximize returns on their aggregate investment expenditures, they are faced with only one constraint: the need to equate at the margin their return from alternative investment opportunities, including those in human capital. (This, of course, should take into account the nontransferability of most investments in human capital, but in essence they are no different from any other form of investment.)

In practice, this process of maximizing alternative investments has to be carried out within a specific institutional framework with its built-in structure of subsidies and the like for different kinds of investment; therefore the maximization process is also constrained by these considerations. Since expected income from investment is partially based on subjective evaluation, the amount that people want to invest in the various alternatives open to them tends to vary from one individual to another. Labor mobility is no exception to this. Nevertheless, in an imperfect market system, assisting labor mobility might prove to be very effective in counteracting some of these imperfections. Moreover, rapid technological change may impose a very heavy burden on many workers. Aiding labor mobility could be viewed, then, as a form of social insurance against this type of hardship, thus distributing the burden on a more nearly equal basis.

A worker might find himself unemployed, underemployed or even unemployable only because of the particular labor market to which he has to relate. In a different labor market, he might find his skill very much in demand. Quite often a worker could not only increase his own productivity by moving to another labor market, but could help to increase the productivity of other workers in the new location. After all, different kinds of labor are, in many instances,

101

complementary in production. Bottlenecks in the supply of certain skills may generate unemployment of other skills. This explains the importance of analyzing gross migration figures rather than using net figures, for cross movements are important.

Even if there were unemployed workers in the demand labor market, it does not mean they can always be transferred to the available jobs, at least not in the short-run and without some sort of retraining. As L. Sjaasted has suggested, if a region has both low and high wage industries, it is not always possible to transfer workers from one group of industries to the other and both out- and in-migration might be necessary.[1] This is a very important point to bear in mind, because there has been considerable resistance—often ill-founded—in this country to aid migration to areas where unemployment exists, which implicitly assumes that labor is homogeneous. Such migration would be inadvisable only if the migrants have the same level of skill as the unemployed workers in the receiving area.

Assisting labor mobility has to be treated both as an independent manpower development tool and an integral part of a comprehensive manpower development program. In some instances, relocation might be the only thing a worker needs to become more productive; but sometimes he might need relocation in conjunction with other manpower development tools, such as retraining. The fact is that quite often relocation is the factor that can make other manpower development tools effective. For example, even a retrained worker may fail to find employment locally, but with mobility assistance he might find a job. That is, without the latter, the investment in the former may not yield a return. This is particularly important in the case of economic minorities because, as discussed earlier, labor market rehabilitation might need a rather comprehensive manpower development program. This is a problem that seems to be present in depressed areas where oftentimes workers are retrained in the expectation of attracting jobs that do not materialize.

Similarly, labor mobility assistance should not be viewed as a mutually exclusive alternative to other economic development tools, such as capital mobility. Quite often they turn out to be complementary. As noted earlier, they represent assistance to different adjustment mechanisms which are not necessarily mutually exclusive. For instance, capital might be considering a move into a depressed area where basically only unskilled labor is available. In-migration of some skilled labor might be absolutely necessary if capital is to move at all. Again, this is very relevant for economic minorities, since both capital and labor mobility can be of help to them and, in the absence of assistance, they are usually among those left behind.

One of the most remarkable things about labor mobility assistance is that it can be used to combat all major forms of unemployment, though this does not mean it is necessarily equally helpful in all cases. Moreover, it can be used during periods of prosperity as well as during periods of recession. In this connection E. and K. Koziara have suggested, for example, that when further increases in aggregate demand might prove to be inflationary, relocation can still fight unemployment.[2] Extreme care should be exercised, however, regarding how much migration is encouraged during recessions, for it is possible that workers whose skills will be again needed as soon as recovery sets in may be needlessly encouraged to migrate. This may prove disequilibrating. Encouragement should be available to those who are not likely to find employment even during prosperity, or whose average productivity would be increased by migration.

At the very least, free market information should be provided to everyone on an equal basis, although in the case of economic minorities, it is likely that this proves insufficient in most instances. It is interesting to note that the development of a job bank and a communication network are top priorities in the transformation of the U.S. Employment Service into a manpower agency. This should help clear the labor market more expeditiously. Provision of such information is a scarce economic resource and acquiring it is a form of investment from which individuals expect to profit, but in this case making it readily available to all could greatly increase the overall performance of the market mechanism with a minimum of interference, a problem so important to the proper functioning of this nation's industrial society.

In addition to this, assistance should be available to help finance labor mobility where it could reduce unemployment and/or increase productivity. Of course, the mobility assistance that would be required in assisting economic minorities is likely to be rather complex, particularly in the case of culturally disadvantaged groups, because mobility assistance has to be supplemented by a wide range of specialized supportive services if such a program is to be effective.

While workers should be expected to repay such assistance to the extent that they benefit directly from migration, in conformity with the underlying philosophy of this work, society should pay for the indirect benefits it might receive in the process. This is a situation where social benefits are more than likely to outweigh private benefits, at least in an advanced industrial setting subject to frequent major technological changes. Many difficulties exist in deciding where direct benefits end and indirect ones begin. This is, however, a subject for research.

Labor mobility assistance would be particularly important if some form of guaranteed income is finally instituted; unemployed workers would not only be producing zero but, in addition society would be supporting them and, as suggested earlier, some of them could be employed and become self-supporting by merely broadening the frontiers of their effective labor market, rather than be forced to take a government created job, as is currently being suggested. A guaranteed income program and a more standardized social security structure would also aid mobility which may be currently hindered, if only partially, by the very significant interstate differences in programs and requirements to qualify.

Labor mobility assistance in combination with adequate labor market information and a job bank should reduce any unnecessary mobility and the chances of perverse mobility since it ought to be borne in mind that the American labor force is reasonably responsive concerning mobility. In the particular case of economic minorities, however, labor mobility assistance would have to be paid *in toto* by society. The very condition of economic minorities precludes them from investing in this form of human capital regardless of its direct profitability. One qualification to the above position should be stated here, however. Society's responsibility to provide free the necessary means for relocation should be limited to what is actually needed to accomplish this objective. Anything given above and beyond this should be subject to the same rules suggested above for labor mobility in general.

The autonomous average propensity of the labor force to migrate is an important variable to take into account in establishing relocation programs. This propensity to migrate is likely to differ from one group of workers to another and from one region to another.[3] This, of course, reflects the investment nature of most migration. It is natural that, *ceteris paribus*, the younger a person is, the more years he has to profit from this investment. Skilled workers tend to have more lateral mobility than semiskilled ones due to the structure of the internal labor market of firms to which reference has already been made. The market for professionals and technical personnel tends to be, on the average, more nationally oriented than most markets for less skilled workers. These are but a few of the factors that will tend to make this form of investment more or less profitable. It should be pointed out, however, that labor mobility assistance, if necessary, might try to alter the pattern of voluntary migration through its subsidy machinery, by encouraging migration that might not otherwise occur.

To show the significance of the average propensity to migrate, suppose the average propensity to migrate of a given set of workers is relatively high, relative to what might be necessary to optimize resource allocation. In this instance, the problem may be more one of directing would-be migrants than of increasing migration so as to avoid a perverse and/or disequilibrating pattern of migration. On the other hand, if the average propensity to migrate is relatively low, relocation programs would have to help overcome this inertia. Obviously, the latter is somewhat more difficult; it is relatively easier to direct movement than to induce it, particularly in view of the self-imposed constraint of permitting maximum freedom of choice within the context of the market system.

Since in the preceding section it was noted that American labor is, on the average, reasonably mobile, it does appear that the problem this nation faces in setting up mobility assistance programs is closer to the former than to the latter situation. In the case of the most disadvantaged—culturally speaking—economic minorities, a little of the latter might have something to recommend it, that is help to overcome inertia, since in this case inertia may reflect the way in which the present institutional framework has adversely affected them and not necessarily a natural unwillingness to move. However, it is important that any effort in this direction be made while providing maximum individual and family freedom.

This approach does provide then an excellent opportunity to more nearly equalize access to the market place and economic opportunity, particularly as an integral part of a comprehensive manpower development strategy. Doing away with the ghetto-slum type of environment in America should be one of the greatest priorities on this country's agenda. Even if the rehabilitation of these areas were at all possible, and doubt seems to be great in this respect, mobility assistance programs can still help to shorten the time it might take to complete the task. Furthermore, if the rehabilitation of these areas turns out to be workable, such programs might help them to obtain types of labor which might be in short supply. However, this latter possibility seems remote at present, to say the least.

Most European countries have for years supported migration programs as part of their manpower development kit. Relocation allowances, family allowances, housing subsidies, counseling, and various supportive services are made available to unemployed workers—and sometimes employed ones—who want to move from areas of high unemployment to areas of low unemployment. In some cases, workers are not even required to have a job lined up in order to receive relocation assistance. Usually, migration can be complemented with retraining, but this is not always the case. In some countries, considerable job information is made available to the workers. However, the provision of housing has proved to be one of the most important factors of all.

The study of the European experience is a very valuable undertaking, though its analysis is beyond the scope of this study. However, there are serious difficulties in transplanting their experience to the American scene without due consideration for this country's needs and institutional characteristics. European mobility programs are part and parcel of their overall manpower development strategies, which are not always compatible with market principles or with the social values held in this country. For example, in some countries it is possible to deny permits to build new factories in areas of low unemployment. Also some of their programs are tied to vocational programs that start early in high school and even in elementary school in some instances. In at least one country, it is mandatory for employers to channel their job openings through the government employment service.

The United States has not yet institutionalized labor mobility assistance programs, that is programs to encourage geographical mobility. So far, Congress has been rather reluctant to spend money for such a purpose. This might be surprising at first, for this country is supposedly operating in a market economy where factor mobility is an important consideration. Moreover, Congress has been prepared to subsidize capital migration in order to alleviate unemployment, and retraining and other manpower development policies might be wasteful, in many instances, if they are not accompanied by relocation. However, it is somewhat less surprising when one realizes that many states and local politicians are afraid to lose their constituency and tax base. Of particular significance is their not unfounded fears that younger people are more inclined to migrate, leaving behind older workers.

Not one of the manpower development acts passed during the 1960s was concerned with this problem; however, a very liberal interpretation of the MDTA has facilitated the use of some funds for E&D mobility projects—that is the rubric of experimentation has been used to circumvent legislative opposition.

The analysis of current efforts with regard to labor mobility schemes suffers from one serious limitation. Current efforts in this area are not only experimental in nature, but they also tend to vary considerably from one program to another; therefore, only the most salient features will be discussed here. So far, 61 projects have been conducted covering some 14,000 workers and their families and encompassing all kinds of groups including economic minorities from urban as well as rural areas.

It seems that supporting manpower development services have been very important in determining the success of the operation. This has been particularly true in the case of economic minorities. Actually, it is rather clear that the lower skill and/or income groups need a relatively greater amount of supporting services. Although this tends to increase the cost of the program, it can be viewed as part of the rehabilitation process discussed in the first part of this study. Moreover, most of these supporting services would have to be provided anyhow in connection with other needs of these families.

It is important to understand that many of the would-be relocatees are quite unfamiliar with what to expect in the new areas. They need help to reorganize their homes once they move to the demand areas. To some extent, this need arises from the very condition of being economic minorities. It is true that other people have relocated without any specific aid, but what is intended here is, first, to induce the migration of some of these people and, second, to get them to move to where they might be needed and accepted. Many of the demand areas are not the old industrial centers; in many instances, they are medium size cities. This is a very welcome development since it helps alleviate the present urban crisis.

The typical staff of one such relocation project (the North Carolina project) serves to illustrate the wide range of services involved: center director, assistant director, housing specialist, job developer, counselor, resident manager for boarding house, and some VISTA volunteers. In the Missouri experiment, for example, the mobility representative assisted relocatees in: securing furniture, moving bids, inspecting applicant's vehicle and insurance, and in what to expect in various phases of their new life.

In all the programs, a job offer is required for the mobility assistance machinery to be set into motion; therefore, in some programs, job development has turned out to be a significant feature. (However in a few instances it has been possible to refer a person for employment after moving to the new location.) This is particularly important in the case of economic minorities, because even when jobs are available in the demand areas, members of economic minorities may find it hard to qualify for them; hence, job developers try to get jobs to be modified to the needs of their clients. In urban projects, the idea of CEP, discussed earlier, has been tried in conjunction with mobility projects.

In addition to a job offer existing, programs require that candidates for relocation assistance be unemployed or partially so and have no reasonable expectation of finding full-time employment locally. Furthermore, they require that jobs available in the demand area could not be filled with qualified local workers, or by local workers who could be trained, or by relocation of nearby workers. These are rather stringent rules which reflect partly an inadequate understanding of the interrelation of various manpower policies and partly the attitude of Congress. The implication of these rules, if literally applied, is that relocation assistance is to be used only as a policy of last resort.

It seems that participants who have received retraining under the MDTA have been relatively more successful than other participants. Success is generally measured by a combination of gains in earnings, stability of employment and desire to stay rather than return to the old location. This suggests that, at least in some cases, relocation is a highly desirable complement of retraining and that the latter without the former might be of little avail.[4]

Another important development is that after resettlement, former seasonal workers and low wage workers tend to be very inclined to stay in the demand area. This reflects probably their greater stability of employment after relocation.

An important feature of these experiments in labor mobility assistance has been the pre-employment interview. First, in most instances employers simply will not hire people they cannot interview. This is especially true in the case of economic minorities. Second, it seems that giving would-be relocatees a chance to visit the demand area has been of great value in encouraging them to participate. In some programs, the spouse is encouraged to travel with the candidate. This adds to the short term cost of the program, but by reducing substantially the chance of failure, it tends to reduce costs in the long run. In a democratic social organization, people simply cannot be forced either to move or to stay regardless of the rationale.

Housing seems to have been one of the most difficult challenges facing relocation programs. This might have been anticipated, for the current housing crisis is nationwide. In the case of economic minorities, some degree of discrimination seems to compound the problem. In this connection, A. Freedman has pointed out the great difficulties involved in arranging moves from ghettos to suburban industrial areas or satellite towns; among other things, due to inadequate social services given their needs.[5] Ghetto dwellers fear discrimination by residents of the demand areas, especially where housing is concerned. To the extent that the housing problem economic minorities confront is part of a national housing crisis, the Swedish policy of making trailers available on a loan basis might prove of some value. Another alternative might be to allow would-be relocatees to apply for public housing, except that in many areas, waiting lists are very long already.[a]

Fortunately, it appears that much relocation has been to areas where the housing problem is somewhat less critical. Nevertheless this is a problem on which labor mobility assistance officials will have to work hardest, for preventing the growth of new slums and ghettos is a must. The ability of an area to absorb people, not only into its labor market, is an important consideration when inducing migration, at least within the present institutional framework.

---

[a] It is not the intention of this work to make a case for public housing. We are simply assuming they exist in many areas.

Labor mobility assistance includes the cost involved in relocating the worker and his family, transportation costs for the family and their belongings, a relocation allowance to smooth out the transition period while the family is settling down, and some incidentals. Usually, it is paid out in several installments. For economic minorities, it is essential that the transitional allowance be sufficient to assist the family to establish themselves at a minimum level of decency. If the allowance is merely token, relocation projects for economic minorities are bound to fail for they do not have the means to finance a move. In the Missouri program, for example, the maximum allowance for a family of four is $280. (The allowance may be increased somewhat if the family cannot find housing.) In the programs studied by W. Mirengoff, the average cost of relocation, including all phases, was under $800.[6] This is in line with an average cost of approximately $850 reported recently by the U.S. Department of Labor.[7] Other studies have reported an average cost of under $400.[b]

In the North Carolina project, selected heads of household were given up to $1,500 to be applied to the purchase of a house and up to $200 towards the purchase of a car.[8] The latter may be important where lack of transportation might prevent a candidate from obtaining a job. But the former raises some serious questions. For one thing, if lack of adequate housing is the problem, other means should be explored before such a policy is instituted. Only if the intention is to help candidates obtain a loan without any subsidization would this practice be less objectionable, and only as long as these programs are just experimental, otherwise more research would be needed as to possible solutions.

With respect to the financing of relocation, while the general feeling seems to be that loans are not good substitutes for grants, this seems to be clearly evident only in the case of economic minorities. Even here, grants are justified without reservation only to cover the minimum amount of expenditures required for a family to complete a relocation. Above and beyond this minimum cost, and in all other cases, either grants or subsidized loans are justifiable only to the extent that the social benefits from relocation appear to exceed private benefits. An unsubsidized system of loans may have something to recommend it, even if the above conditions are not satisfied, when the encouragement of labor mobility is considered an important national goal.

It is apparent that, in principle, labor mobility programs would result in benefits to both demand and supply areas; hence, some form of cooperation between them regarding social security and the like would seem desirable given our present institutional framework. This is likely to become a much more serious issue if workers are encouraged to migrate without having a job lined up. The issue of cooperation presents, however, a very difficult practical problem. Areas experiencing relatively large losses of population through assisted relocation are likely to be uncooperative. But, a federally-sponsored system of guaranteed income could go a long way toward solving the problem now posed by interstate variations.

---

[b]Variations are to be expected since the programs differ in at least three important respects: type of assistance provided, group composition and average distance involved.

There have been some returnees. They are usually referred to as 'relocation failures'. The reasons given for returning cover a wide spectrum. They vary, of course, with the background and other personal characteristics of the individual such as rural or city, age, family, etc. In the Missouri program, there was a very interesting development. The characteristics of withdrawing applicants and returnees were found to be not too different. This might suggest that in a given group, relocatees with characteristics similar to that of withdrawing candidates are more likely to become relocation failures, and measures could be undertaken to minimize the incidence of failure.

Also, in most programs, the incidence of returns seems to be higher among disadvantaged groups. The reasons for this seem evident. But, as was suggested earlier, there is some evidence that among seasonal workers, low paid workers, and trainees from MDT programs, the chances of success are above average. Also, there is a relatively greater chance of success when men are accompanied by their wives and families than when they move alone. All this suggest areas for research and improvement.

This author would recommend that labor mobility assistance programs for all who can benefit be finally incorporated into this nation's manpower development strategies during the next decade, and that they include special provisions for economic minorities. Also that they be available separately or as part of a general manpower development strategy which, if his prescription is followed, would be conceived as part of an overall economic security strategy.

10 The Resettlement Program for Cuban National Refugees

This section presents an analysis of the resettlement program established by the United States government to assist Cuban National Refugees (CNR). It is not concerned, however, with other aspects of the overall CNR program, except to the extent that might be necessary for an adequate understanding of the resettlement program.

It is the largest such program currently in existence, since the experimental program for American families is still relatively small, as was noted in the preceding section. The study of this program provides a rare opportunity for analyzing the potential and problems of mobility programs as a manpower development tool. It deals with a group of people that, for the most part, are impoverished upon arrival in this country, a group that has to make a major social adjustment and overcome a language and cultural barrier, and who upon resettlement frequently has to make a second adjustment, sometimes under rather adverse conditions.

The analysis will be developed against the background of extensive field work conducted by the author for this purpose. First, the methodology used in gathering the data will be explained. Second, the need and major objectives of the program will be discussed. Finally, the evidence will be examined from the point of view of its value to manpower development.

Methodology

Extensive use was made of the questionnaire technique in the collection of information pertaining to CNR involved in the resettlement program. This technique was deemed appropriate given the nature of the research, for many of the factors had to be evaluated subjectively by the people affected. Sampling was an absolute necessity due to the sheer size of the relevant population in relation to the resources available for this purpose.

In the belief that the experience of a given subset of resettled CNR could be of great value, an attempt was made to study a sub-program. Moreover, the names and relocation addresses of participants in the resettlement program as a whole were not available. This ruled out any attempt to use randomnization. An area of the United States was sought where a relatively large number of CNR have been resettled. In making the selection, large metropolitan areas were ruled out. First, a considerable number of the people who resettle in these areas are only nominally part of the resettlement program. Second, resettlement to these areas is not given high priority. In general manpower development programs in the United States are trying to avoid adding to the many problems already confronted by many large metropolitan areas.

The area selected was a medium-size city with a population of approximately 175,000 in 1960. (It was agreed not to disclose the name of the area.) It was possible to obtain the cooperation of the participants in the resettlement effort to this area, including the major liaison group in it. It was fortunate that participants in this sub-program are fairly representative of the resettled CNR population as a whole, as evidenced later.

A second sample was developed through the following channel. Cuban national refugees have, for the most part, organized themselves in exile along municipal lines based on where they lived before leaving their homeland. It was possible to obtain the participation of a fairly large sample of resettled CNR who originally came to this country from one such municipality. It was anticipated that this second sample would provide some cross-sectional information about the resettlement program comprising, as it did, resettled families from all over the country.

The hypothesis that the two samples came from the same economic population in Cuba was tested. The F test[1] was used to test the hypothesis. Current income of heads of household was used as a proxy for economic background. The hypothesis was rejected at the 99 percent level of confidence, thus it is statistically likely that the members of the two samples came, on the average, from different economic backgrounds. A similar test was run using the income of heads of household after arrival in the United States, but before resettlement. The hypothesis that they came from the same economic population was rejected at the 95 percent confidence level, but not at the 99 percent confidence level. This finding seems quite reasonable, for on arrival, most CNR had to accept any available job while learning English and adjusting to the new environment; hence, any skill they might have possessed would probably not have shown in their income.

Field work was also used extensively to obtain specific information. Interviews were conducted with personnel in some of the government agencies involved in the assistance program for CNR. Also, some of the sponsors of specific sub-programs were interviewed. All this was greatly facilitated by the author's first-hand familiarity with the program.

The information gathered, particularly through the questionnaires, was quite extensive. In general, an effort was made to obtain information on the participants' background (including financial), the effect that the resettlement experience seems to have had on them, particularly from the manpower point of view, and the major characteristics of the program. The questions were prepared so that some cross references were available. This was expected to help in determining the reliability of the replies. Moreover, indirect means of establishing the actual attitude of the participants were used whenever possible.

The number of questionnaires mailed out was 80 and 75 respectively. Approximately 65 to 70 percent were returned in each sample. The family was the unit of study and heads of household were asked to fill out the questionnaires. Unattached individuals were treated as one-member units; however, there were very few cases of unattached individuals. The number of replies obtained varied from question to question. This was due to two factors: first, some people failed to answer one or more questions; second, the questions did not always apply to all members of the household.

The Resettlement Program: Need and Objectives

The influx of CNR to this country started in 1959, but did not reach alarming proportions until 1961. For reasons beyond the scope of this study, CNR have shown a strong preference for the Miami and surrounding areas. This was preferred, at least for some time, even at the price of a reduced standard of living relative to what could have been attained by moving to other labor markets. The following figures suggest the labor market impact of the influx as well as its major fluctuations:

	Arrivals	*Resettlements*[a]
February 1961 to October 1962	153,534	48,361
October 1962 to December 1965	29,962	46,547
December 1965 to December 1968	125,672	110,986
	309,168	205,894

Despite the remarkable effort made by CNR to become financially independent, for example, by seeking opportunities outside the area, the impact on the labor market was very considerable. Making matters worse was the relatively high unemployment level afflicting the American economy in general at the turn of the last decade (1958-1962), and the structure of the economy of the Miami area. Such an influx was bound to cause some friction with those local workers most directly affected by the entrance of CNR into the local labor force.

This situation represented a major test of the ability of the labor market to absorb a large influx of labor under rather adverse conditions. It was under this set of circumstances that the U.S. government decided to establish programs to assist new arrivals. At first, emergency funds were allocated largely to alleviate the pressure on local welfare agencies. Then in 1962, Congress passed the "Migration and Refugee Assistance Act". The act contains three major features of manpower interest:

a) it provides assistance to state and local public agencies providing services for substantial numbers of individuals who meet the requirements of the act for health, education and employment training purposes;

---

[a]These are official resettlements as reported by the U.S. Department of Health, Education, and Welfare, Social and Rehabilitation Services, Washington, D.C.

    b) it provides for transportation to, and resettlement in other areas of the United States for individuals who meet the requirements of the act and who need assistance in obtaining such services;

    c) it provides for the establishment and maintenance of projects for employment of refresher professional training of individuals who meet the requirements of the act.

Take note (b) is directly concerned with resettlement which is the central theme of this second part of the study; (a) and (c) are also clear cases of manpower development in action. It should be noted, too, that the resettlement effort began before the passage of this act, as the figures above suggest (48,361 resettled in the period February 1961 to October 1962). During the interim period, the program was financed through the emergency funds already referred to. Passage of the act simply served to institutionalize the program.

It is clear, then, that the major objective of the program was, and still is, to assist CNR widen their labor market horizon by helping them to resettle where jobs were relatively more plentiful. In so doing, it was also taking some of the pressure off the Miami and vicinity labor market. The remaining CNR could then be absorbed by the local labor market in a more orderly fashion. This suggests the potentiality of manpower development in assisting the market to perform better.

For reasons beyond the scope of this study, there was a very considerable slowdown in the number of arrivals between October 1962 and December 1965. This made it possible for resettlement to exceed arrivals, thus reducing the absolute number of CNR in the Miami area. In this regard, until December of 1965, the resettlement program remained technically a voluntary matter, though considerable pressure was brought to bear upon CNR to participate.

The major weapon used to get people to participate was the threatened loss of financial assistance if they remained in the Miami area. However, there were many who truly volunteered for resettlement. In passing, it is interesting to note that a similar high pressure form of persuasion was incorporated into the 1967 amendment to the Social Security Act, as noted earlier in this study; it will also be part, if passed by Congress, of the family assistance program proposed by President Nixon.

Since December 1965, two resettlement policies have been pursued. For those who arrived in this country prior to this date voluntarism still is the major approach. For those who came after December 1965, however, resettlement to the location of the sponsor is automatic.[b] Refusal to relocate carries with it the loss of financial assistance which is only available in the place of resettlement. This financial assistance is paid by the federal government through the local welfare agency in the place of resettlement. This policy applies only to those coming through the airlift, however. For those who either have not come through the airlift or whose sponsors happen to live in the Miami area,

[b]The sponsor is the person who supports the application to enter this country of new arrivals coming through the airlift.

voluntarism is also the policy. Because the influx of CNR through the airlift between December of 1965 and the present has been substantial, arrivals have outnumbered resettlements. However, the pressure on the labor market has not been so great as it was during the early part of the 1960s, in part because of the greater experience in dealing with the problem.

It seems relevant at this point to comment on the assistance provided to CNR in the Miami area. This will give some indication of the pressure that has always existed to relocate outside this area when jobs cannot be found. Cuban national refugees receive basically the same quality and quantity of assistance received by other members of the Miami area who qualify for assistance. This includes the standard items, like payments in kind and in cash, counseling, health services, educational services, and some miscellaneous items.

The welfare program in the Miami area, however, has never been known as a liberal one, which suggests that CNR receiving assistance in this area have for the most part never lived much above subsistence level. The average monthly welfare cost per person has been in the neighborhood of $35 to $40. It could be expected then that such levels of assistance would have encouraged CNR to participate in relocation programs and, as was seen, many of them did so even during the entirely voluntary stage of the program.

The Demand Areas

It is relevant here to discuss types of areas where CNR have been resettling. The number of American cities that have received CNR at one time or another is staggering. As of December of 1969, the number was 2,541. This includes cities of all kinds and sizes. Obviously, in quite a few cases the number of resettlements is really small. However, in the case of 102 cities (excluding metropolitan areas) 100 or more persons have been involved. These 102 cities are of great interest to this study for they are, for the most part, cities where sub-programs have been established by private groups (sponsors) of various kinds in order to give special assistance to relocatees.[c]

There has been a marked tendency to establish these sub-programs in areas whose population has been expanding. In only 16 out of the 102 cities receiving over 100 persons did the population decline between 1950 and 1960. There has also been a tendency to resettle people in industrialized areas. For example, in 65 of these 102 cities manufacturing accounted for at least 20 percent of total employment in 1960 (metropolitan areas are not included). Not entirely unrelated to the above two characteristics, these cities are also among those having relatively high median family incomes. In 1960 a large majority of them had median family incomes of over $6,000; only in a very few instances was it under $4,800.

It is impossible to analyze here all the labor markets involved. However, the

---

[c]The role of these private groups (sponsors) will be discussed at some length at a later stage of this study.

evidence lends some support to the view that, on the average, the relocation or 'demand' areas are expanding centers with relatively high median family incomes, hence in a relatively better position to accommodate newcomers. In cases where this has not been so, highly specialized labor has frequently been involved, therefore, tending to make a contribution to the area. This is relevant to manpower development analysis, for it is important to assist people to move to areas where ample opportunities exist, and where they will not harm the chances of local labor to find employment.

Cuban National Refugees: Their Background

It is necessary to explore some of the major characteristics of the refugee population for there seems to be some misconception about it in this country. The evidence available is unfortunately very limited in scope and covers only the period from December 1965 to the present.

A widespread notion held in this country is that most CNR come from high income families. No data are available on income, but some are available on the occupational structure of the refugee population which can throw some light on this issue.

Table 10-1 suggests that the number of people with some form of skill is considerable, but they are not the overwhelming majority. For example, the category clerical and sales, the largest, includes many workers who do not possess a high level of skill.[d] In addition, those grouped under professional include a substantial number of semi-professional, technical and kindred workers, whose skills are relatively high, but who are not likely to come from families with very high incomes in Cuba. It will be noted that the category which includes housewives is very large. One reason for this is that the labor force

Table 10-1
Occupational Structure of the CNR Population (December 1965 to March 1970)

Professional, semi-professional, technical	6.5%
Clerical and sales	11.7
Skilled	9.3
Semi-skilled	3.6
Service	1.7
Farm and fishing	1.7
Children, students and housewives	64.0

Source: U.S. Department of Health, Education, and Welfare, Social and Rehabilitation Services, Washington, D.C.

---

[d]This classification was on the basis of occupations followed in Cuba. The occupational structure of developing countries is not easy to compare to that of the United States, but for the present purpose this should not pose any major problem.

participation of women in developing countries is relatively much lower than in advanced industrial societies like the United States. Moreover, a considerable number of women came alone in order to take their children out of Cuba.[e] This author knows that the student group includes relatively few men between the ages of 14 and 27; young men are generally not allowed to leave Cuba due to their military obligations.

Finally, it is significant to indicate that if data were available for the period prior to December of 1965, it is likely that the average level of skill of the refugee population would be somewhat higher than that suggested by the above figures. The evidence from our two samples supports the view that the average quality of manpower prior to this date was relatively somewhat higher than that of the manpower arriving thereafter.

Table 10-2 suggests that the age distribution of the refugee population follows the same pattern of distribution of the American population as a whole; slightly under 60 percent are between the ages of 18 and 65. The proportion of the U.S. population between the ages of 16 and 65 was approximately 60 percent in 1970. (This is as close as the available data come to the group of working age.) The only unusual thing that can be observed in table 10-2 is the relatively low figure for those between the ages of 18 and 29, resulting from the above mentioned policy of the Cuban government concerning military service.

There are no data available, unfortunately, on the racial composition of the refugee population, but it is the experience of this author that all racial groups are represented. The racial composition of the refugee population is likely to follow rather closely that of the Cuban population at large.

All of the above evidence will be greatly supplemented through the data to be discussed at a later stage in this section, including data on schooling which are not available for the entire refugee population.

Table 10-2
Age Distribution of the CNR Population (December 1965 to March 1970)

Age Group		Age Group	
0–5	11.3%	40–50	15.7%
6–18	22.8	50–60	10.5
19–29	8.9	60–65	4.1
30–39	19.4	65 +	7.3

Source: U.S. Department of Health, Education, and Welfare, Social and Rehabilitation Services, Washington, D.C.

---

[e]In 1967 out of an approximate refugee population in Dade county (Florida) of 208,000 some 20,600 (or 10 percent) were school children.[2]

Resettlement Assistance

The resettlement assistance consists of: a) transportation for the entire family, b) a transitional resettlement allowance equivalent to one month's cash assistance, c) some clothing, d) the cost of moving household goods, and e) some miscellaneous items related to relocation. In general, counseling services are available too. It should be pointed out that the cost of moving household goods is relatively small, for CNR have, on the average, very few belongings before relocation. Actually, in the case of those who are resettled as part of the airlift, this cost is almost non-existent. On the other hand, the need for clothing is relatively great; but most of this clothing is obtained through the work of the several private agencies through which the resettlement effort is channeled—private non-profit organizations which assist the U.S. Department of Health, Education, and Welfare to administer the entire refugee program. The assistance does not include any private aid, as sometimes provided by these private agencies in place of relocation. This aid will be discussed later.

It is significant to note that the resettlement assistance given to CNR has not differed appreciably from the resettlement assistance given to American families under the experimental relocation program discussed in the preceding section. The experimental nature of the latter, however, has permitted some greater latitude—something that has not been possible under the more structured program for CNR where expediency has been important. This suggests the important pioneering role played by the resettlement program.

The average cost of resettling CNR was approximately $140 per person in 1968. This was expected to increase to about $150 by 1970. This author has estimated that this average cost rises to the neighborhood of $165 to $170 when the cost of administering the program is taken into account. (This does not include private assistance, however.) This means that the average resettlement cost for a family of four has been approximately between $600 and $700. There is, of course, considerable variation depending upon the point of final destination of the relocatees. (The average cost of relocation may have been somewhat higher prior to December of 1965 due to the relatively greater number of relocatees who had been residing in the Miami area for some time and had acquired more belongings.) These average cost figures are very much in line with those in the experimental program for American families, which is not surprising in view of the similarities of these two programs.

Once the relocation process is completed, the responsibility of the program towards the individual and his family ceases. Relocatees are entitled to apply for local assistance if and when needed, but they are subject to the rules governing the local welfare of their new place of residence. Relocatees who return to the Miami area receive, for the most part, the same treatment given to American families who wish to establish their residence there.

Only about 8 percent of the resettled CNR who have come to this country through the airlift are currently receiving welfare. It should be borne in mind, however, that these people are expected to resettle immediately upon their arrival in this country; yet, language and other problems of adjustment might mean some delay in entering their first jobs. Moreover, some of them are older people who cannot enter the job market. The average monthly cost of this assistance in 1968 was $78 per needy resettled CNR.[f] Of course, some state and local aid is also available in some instances, but only as they are absorbed locally.

Sub-program Resettlement

To be eligible for resettlement assistance, a would-be relocatee needs a sponsor and/or a job offer. In the case of those coming through the airlift, having a sponsor is a prerequisite for coming to this country; however, for other CNR this has not been so, at least not in practice. For this latter group, it has not been easy to meet the sponsor/job requirement, particularly during the first few years of the program. The vast majority lacked the contacts. Yet, the chief objective of the program was, and still is, to get CNR to resettle outside the Miami area. (This is a paradox also encountered in American manpower policies, whereby people in areas with relatively excessive labor are told of jobs and opportunity in other areas, and yet are not given assistance to make the move.)

To bridge this gap, the voluntary agencies, through which the program has been channeled, made an effort from the beginning to serve either as sponsors or as liaisons with other sponsors. This liaison service has also been extended in practice to many of the airliftees who are resettled automatically. These voluntary agencies were also making available an important intangible asset in short supply, namely expertise in helping people.

The sponsoring process has been greatly aided through the contacts made by many of the participants in the first wave of relocations both on an individual as well as on a group basis. Sponsors try to find employers with unfilled vacancies who are willing to make a job offer, then conduct all the necessary arrangements for the completion of the operation. They have also been willing, at times, to assume full responsibility for relocatees, and once in the new location, they have tried to find jobs for them. This proved very valuable at the beginning of the program for it was soon discovered that there were many CNR willing to benefit from this opportunity.

The resettlement program does not have funds for pre-relocation exploratory trips, whereby relocatees are enabled to visit the demand area and be interviewed by would-be employers, such as are available for American families in the experimental relocation program discussed earlier. This suggests the important role played by the voluntary agencies in filling partially this gap in the resettlement program. They are in an excellent position to help remove some of the obstacles in the way of newcomers who are attempting to establish a new home for themselves and their families. It is this author's belief that this kind of voluntary agency could play a very important role in the manpower develop-

---

[f]Information is available on the airlift group because their welfare payments are made out of federal funds, though administered locally.

ment of economic minorities in general, especially if the problem is to be viewed realistically and the job is to be done. After all, they do have the power to unlock many doors in the path of economic minorities, particularly in the job and housing markets.

Other Manpower Development Assistance

The Migration and Refugee Assistance Act provides for other forms of manpower development, particularly to help professional people use their skills at the earliest possible date. This reflects concern over the waste of such valuable assets. Scores of professional people have received some form of aid along these lines. In doing this, frequently retraining has been the key feature, as when professionals have been retrained to teach Spanish or do social work or library work.[g] Accompanying this effort has been the provision of supportive services essential to manpower development, such as health services. The federal government has also made available funds to provide vocational training, adult education, and especially support for the education of children in the Dade County area. Vocational training has been given in such diverse trades as welding, upholstery, keypunching operations, child care, etc. English classes have been extensively provided. In fact in order to qualify for assistance, CNR were expected to enroll in these English classes.

Concerning children, an effort has been made to avoid their having to wait to learn regular subject matter until they learn English.[h] The primary objective of all this has been to speed up the process of adjustment so that adults can become productive, and children can adapt to the new environment in the shortest possible time. Although, it is likely that the major benefits of this policy accrue to Dade County, sometimes this training and better adjustment have proven very valuable on a wider front. After all, they do tend to increase current and future productivity which is of general benefit to the country regardless of the refugees' place of residence. Particularly the English component of the program has enhanced the labor market horizon of many CNR.[i]

There is one program which warrants special mention here because it shows the possible value of circumventing local opposition to the financing of such a program, and because it became a feature of the 1967 Amendment to the Social Security Act. This is the 'Training for Independence' program for women with

[g]It is noteworthy that recently displaced American engineers have been retrained to teach in high schools and colleges.

[h]It is interesting to observe that similar efforts are currently under way in areas with a high concentration of culturally disadvantaged minority groups under existing manpower development programs.

[i]This kind of effort in the case of Americans is hard to synchronize with relocation programs. Local financing is usually heavily relied upon, and areas are generally reluctant to contribute if they anticipate such losses, especially if their population is already declining.

dependent children, a group which forms a sizeable part of the CNR population (see table 10-1). The idea behind this program has been to make these mothers financially independent, for otherwise they simply serve to enlarge the AFDC welfare rolls.

Participation is compulsory. But still more significant, a participant has to sign a statement agreeing to take the training and eventually accept resettlement, if this is necessary for her to find a job. The penalty is the loss of financial assistance.[j] Daycare facilities have been provided to support the operation. Vocational training is combined with language training to increase the chances of finding employment. It is relevant to stress the insistence on linking training with resettlement regardless of how successful this linkage has proved to be in this particular program. This is interesting in view of the general opposition of Congress to embark on any such program for American families. (This is a paradox, not merely because CNR may have been treated differently, but because the potentiality of this mechanism has been recognized in this program and yet, no clear attempt has been made to expand it into our national manpower development programs.)

Only some 200 participants in the Training for Independence program had been resettled by early 1968; however, employment opportunities were relatively high at the time, reducing the need for resettlement. It is possible that the future earnings expected from relocation may not have justified the investment involved in moving, at least not from the individual's point of view. However, it should be emphasized that the kind of rehabilitation undertaken by the sponsors of the program is not the kind envisioned by this author in the first part of this study, for it does not represent rehabilitation in depth. Therefore, the failure or success of the mechanisms the program incorporates, at least in principle, should not be judged in terms of such a short term kind of manpower development.

The Samples

In regard to the information collected through the questionnaires, the sample comprised by those CNR who have moved to the same location in the United States (i.e. members of a sub-program) will be referred to as sample 1. The sample comprised by those CNR who originally lived in the same municipality in Cuba will be referred to as sample 2. Whenever possible, the samples will be used to compare the resettled population with the CNR population at large.

Schooling

The sample data on schooling do not include children; they reflect the level of schooling of relocatees of working age. Moreover, they reflect the level of schooling attained before coming to this country.

---

[j]It will be recalled that this author questioned earlier the use of this high pressure technique in the case of many welfare recipients and very especially, mothers with dependent children. Encouragement and incentives are acceptable; force is objectionable, unless it is shown they really refused to help themselves.

Table 10-3
Years of Schooling of Relocatees

	Sample 1	Sample 2
0 to 4	20	2
5 to 8	10	12
9 to 11	18	17
12 or more	26	38
	74	69

It is clear from the above figures that the average level of schooling of relocatees in sample 2 is higher than that of relocatees in sample 1. (This is consistent with earlier findings that it is unlikely that, on the average, people in sample 1 and sample 2 would have come from the same income population in Cuba since education and income are likely to be positively associated.) It is relevant to point out that in many instances the lack of adequate knowledge of the English language might have served to lower their educational attainments from a practical point of view. Furthermore, it is likely that a given number of years of schooling would prove relatively more advantageous in Cuba than in the United States, because of the existing differences between the two countries in the level of economic development. These two factors could be viewed as forms of labor market downgrading, if only in a relative sense.

Age Composition

In the study of relocation programs the analysis of age composition is important, for it might suggest an above average propensity to participate of certain age groups. The limitations of the data do not permit comparisons with what may be considered the normal pattern of migration, but some suggestions seem possible.

Table 10-4
Age Distribution of Relocatees

	Sample 1	Sample 2
0 to 6	15	7
7 to 16	32	20
17 to 24	14	16
25 to 44	41	38
45 to 55	19	19
56 and over	9	13
	130	113

Generally speaking, the age distribution of the two samples does not differ greatly. The relatively low participation of people in the 17-24 age group seems to be largely attributable to the policy of the Cuban government concerning people of military age.

The age profile of participants in the CNR relocation programs might differ from that of voluntary migration in general. As was explained earlier, age seems to be an important factor influencing the return a person can expect from this form of investment, for it suggests the time he has left to profit from it. This factor seems to be important for participants in relocation programs but to a lesser extent because this form of migration is subsidized.

Relocation programs could be used to encourage migration that might not otherwise take place, thus altering somewhat the age profile of relocatees relative to voluntary migrants. The factor of subsidization is important in the present context, for it seems to have facilitated the relocation of relatively older workers. The figures in table 10-4 suggest that while CNR in the prime age group (22-44), at least from a labor market point of view, have exhibited a high propensity to participate, a rather significant number of CNR over 44 years of age have also taken advantage of the labor market opportunities opened up by participating in the resettlement program. Factors like property ownership are not likely to detract from the willingness to relocate in the case of this group. However, attachment to the local community and group is a more complex issue. On the one hand, they are not living in their regular environment, but on the other hand, the Miami area is, to a considerable extent, regarded as their second homeland.

Another interesting characteristic of the age distribution of the samples is the relatively large number of children. This suggests that married people with families have been very active participants in the program. This is noteworthy, for usually single people, particularly if they are young, have a much higher propensity to migrate than married people. This behavior also suggests the relative importance of relocation assistance. It should also be pointed out that the resettlement program has made an effort to keep families together. This seems to be a very desirable policy in any program involving economic minorities. It was noted earlier that in the experimental program for American families, policies directed to keeping families together seem to have been very rewarding, as reflected in relatively higher retention rates.

Occupational Profile

One of the major manpower objectives of the resettlement program has been to enable people to exploit to the fullest, and as soon as possible, their talents and skills. That CNR were, in most cases, failing to maximize their potential income from work—given their level of skill—was strongly suggested by the fact that the incomes prior to resettlement of people in both samples did not differ significantly, even though it was statistically unlikely that they had come from the same income population in Cuba.

In examining and comparing the occupational profiles in Cuba and in the United States, it is important to bear in mind that possessing a given skill may be of little value in the absence of an adequate knowledge of the English language. Moreover, in some instances, licensing and/or union membership may prove to be a difficult obstacle to overcome in trying to find jobs commensurate with skills. In addition, it is not at all clear how the higher level of development of the American economy may have affected the refugees. While it appears that for some it might have opened up new opportunities as well as a greater choice of jobs, for others technological differences might have been an additional handicap, though many of the techniques of production used in Cuba had been imported from the United States. All this renders any interpretation of the evidence a rather difficult undertaking.

Table 10-5 suggests a marked increased in the relative importance of the blue collar group, particularly the semiskilled sub-group. This seems largely attributable to the following causes: first, some downgrading of skills resulting from the factors previously discussed; second, the entry into the labor force of workers who in some instances lack adequate training. This is the case of some of the housewives who entered the labor force after coming to this country. Finally, it is likely that some workers may have preferred a higher income in a blue collar job to a lower income in a white collar job, particularly in view of the relatively narrow range of choices open to many of them in the white collar sector.[k]

The evidence also suggests that, in quite a few instances, it was possible to remain within the same broad occupational group. This seems to have been particularly true in sample 2 which has a higher average level of educational

Table 10-5
Occupational Profile of Relocatees

	Sample 1		Sample 2	
	In Cuba	In the U.S.	In Cuba	In the U.S.
Blue collar				
Unskilled	5	7	2	2
Semiskilled	6	29	4	14
Skilled	7	9	5	5
White collar				
Office and kindred	14	7	10	16
Technical	7	3	4	7
Professional	7	4	14	7
Self-employed, managers	6	0	6	2
	52	60	45	53

[k]Quite apart from the language barrier, many do not have access to some major sources of white collar jobs; for example, civil service jobs.

attainment. Had they stayed in the Miami area, it is doubtful they would have been able to do this, at least to the same extent. Moreover, it is this author's experience that jobs in new locations tend to offer, on the average, a greater degree of employment stability, particularly in the case of blue collar jobs. This is an additional benefit accruing from relocation.

These gains resulting from relocation point to the considerable losses that may otherwise occur in the form of wasted talent and loss of production, especially at a time when technological development seems to show a certain bias against unskilled and some important types of low skilled white collar jobs. This suggests the significance of resettlement programs in enhancing the marketability of many workers, particularly when they are handicapped in some way and are members of economic minority groups. The evidence provided by these two samples suggests that the resettlement program has been rather successful in achieving this objective in the case of CNR, even though its success cannot be measured adequately.

It seems appropriate at this point to indicate that only 1 person in sample 1 and 3 persons in sample 2 received some kind of formal training after coming to the United States which helped them to find employment. The resettlement program as such does not have any provisions for retraining. However, after relocating, CNR are entitled to participate in most of the manpower development programs available in their new place of residence, and are subject to the same regulations as local people. In addition, relocatees who spent some time in the Miami area may have received some job training there, but prior to resettlement and not in connection with the resettlement effort (with the exception of some professionals and participants in the Training for Independence Program discussed earlier).

Formal education in basic English was received by ten persons in sample 1 and twelve persons in sample 2. This was usually undertaken as part of the requirements to qualify for general assistance in the Miami area (although it was not always required), and has in many instances proved as important as job training. All this is significant, for in the experience of the program for American families, resettlement tends to be, on the average, more effective when the relocatees have participated in some form of retraining program under the MDTA. In the case of CNR, expediency may not have permitted combining training and relocation to the same extent.

Labor Force Status of Women

Manpower analysis is very much concerned with the labor force participation of women. This is significant in the present context for the labor force status of women in the CNR population seems to have undergone a change.

The figures in table 10-6 suggest there has been a quite substantial net increase in the labor force participation of women among resettled CNR in both samples. This is consistent with the general trend in women's labor force

Table 10-6
Changes in the Labor Force Status of Women Relocatees

In Cuba	In the U.S.	Sample 1	Sample 2
From housewife	To housewife	16	15
From housewife	To worker	11	9
From worker	To housewife	2	3
From worker	To worker	14	10
	Net Change:	+9	+6

participation in the United States. It is also consistent with the relatively higher labor force participation among women in economically advanced countries.

This author found that this net increase in women's labor force participation among CNR women has been greatly aided by resettlement. Even though their potential labor force participation in the Miami area might have been similar, a relatively low level of wages and an inadequate supply of suitable jobs there would have prevented many of them from entering the labor market. Inasmuch as the program has succeeded in enhancing the job marketability of the entire family, it has helped some of these families to either lift themselves out of poverty or prevent themselves from falling into it.

It is possible then to see this development as a positive contribution of the resettlement program; however, it is only fair to give some of the credit to the participants for their positive attitude in the above regard. This experience of the resettlement program for CNR should not be overlooked in the establishment of relocation programs for economic minorities in general. Increasing the average labor force participation of the household can be a very important contribution of this sort of program in the battle against poverty. This approach is particularly significant to this study for it is consistent with its underlying philosophy of relying on the market mechanism as much as possible.

Income

Manpower development is usually intended as a means of improving the relative economic position of those exposed to it. Resettlement programs are no exception to this rule. Income is by no means the only index of economic well being; for example, job security, possibilities for advancement, etc. are equally important. Nevertheless, income is usually viewed as the most significant variable. In this connection, it is relevant to examine the effect that the resettlement program seems to have had on the average income of the participants. This study is interested in objective as well as in subjective evaluations. The latter because the success of manpower policies depends partly on what participants think the program has done for them. However, to those who have to decide on the allocation of resources for manpower development, objective evaluations are highly desirable. A word of caution: inasmuch as spatial and intertemporal income comparisons are always difficult to make, extreme care has to be exercised in interpreting the evidence.

The annual current income from work of men was compared to their corresponding income prior to relocation.[1] In all but one case (in sample 1) income had increased substantially. Even after taking into account the growth of the economy during the intervening years, the growth in annual income was still very considerable in most cases. It was not unusual to find that a person of average skill had increased his income by $4,500 to $5,000 over a period of 4 to 5 years. In addition, in many instances, the average annual income from work of other members of the household—particularly women—increased, too, or they were able to enter the labor market. This resulted, of course, in even greater gains when family income is taken into account.

At this juncture, it is relevant to refer again to the finding that when the Miami income was used, no statistically significant difference was found between the two samples regarding financial background, but that when current income was used, the two samples were found to differ. This suggests that labor market conditions in the Miami area, plus other handicaps, were preventing many participants from maximizing their income potential. It appears that relocation enabled participants to make better use of their respective skills, and since the level of educational attainment was, on the average, higher in sample 2 than in sample 1, income differences started to show up again. The objective evidence then supports the view that the program has been successful in improving the allocating of resources.

In relation to the subjective evaluation of participants concerning their financial position, heads of household were asked to state whether, in their own view, their income from work had improved relative to what they could be earning in Miami. The following was the result:

	Sample 1	Sample 2
yes	23	24
no	3	0
not certain	10	9

The above figures suggest that, in both samples, most heads of household felt they were financially better off in their new place of residence than in the Miami area. This evidence also clearly supports the view that the resettlement program has been instrumental in improving the utilization of the talents of most participants.

Returnees

One of the greatest challenges confronting relocation programs in a democratic society is that there is no way to prevent participants, if they so wish, from

---

[1]In a few instances the person involved was never in Miami, therefore, no comparison was possible. However, there are no reasons to believe that their experience would have been any different from that of other people in the samples.

returning to their original location, with consequent loss to the program. As noted earlier, it was possible for greater pressure to be applied on CNR, due to their lack of access to welfare assistance as a matter of right, at least for some time. This is a problem very much feared in the case of economic minorities, for they may feel—sometimes rightly—that they have not been accepted, or that they have not improved their financial position sufficiently to want to stay rather than return to the old environment where they may feel more secure, particularly since rehabilitation in depth is not yet a reality. A widely used measure of the success of relocation programs is the retention rate; that is, the proportion of those who stay in the demand area once the relocation process has been completed. Those who return are viewed as relocation failures. In the experimental program for American families, returning to the original area within a period of 2 to 3 months after the date of relocation is recorded as a failure. However, the establishment of this period has been due largely to the availability of the data.

In discussing the experience of the resettlement program, it is necessary to distinguish among three groups of relocatees who have chosen not to stay in the relocation or demand area. They represent different analytical phenomena for manpower development purposes. First, there are those relocatees who can be considered real failures; they simply did not want to stay in the demand area after completion of the relocation process. This group, in turn, can be divided into two sub-groups: those who have been in the Miami area before, and those who were sent directly to the demand area upon their arrival in this country through the airlift.

The latter sub-group presents an interesting problem: having never lived in Miami, they are in no position to appraise adequately the job market, housing market, etc. of the area. Nevertheless, for them, Miami still represents a familiar environment in this country, and they do have some information through acquaintances.

Second, there are those relocatees who have returned to Miami, but who cannot be considered relocation failures. Some have returned to try to establish a business of their own, which suggests they were able to save a relatively substantial amount of money within a rather short period of time, namely 4 to 5 years, on the average. Others have acquired new skills or have upgraded their old ones, including here the learning of the English language, and in general have become better equipped to compete in the labor market. Relocation has been an effective manpower development tool in their case, for this is one of its major objectives.

Finally, there are those relocatees who have left the demand area but have not returned to Miami. Instead, they have migrated to another area of the country. This usually occurs after they were in the original demand area for a few years and had time to enhance the marketability of their skills. Their situation is rather similar to that of the second group in the sense that they cannot be considered relocation failures.

Unfortunately, no ongoing record has been kept on relocatees, since the responsibility of the U.S. government ceases with relocation; therefore, no official data exist on relocation failures. This has made it necessary to rely on information provided by the relocatees in the samples, and by some of the people assisting in the relocation process. The most widely quoted figure of those leaving the relocation area fell between 15 percent to 20 percent of all relocatees. However, only a very few of these seem to have returned to the Miami area shortly after relocation. It appears that approximately one-half of those who have left did not go back to the Miami area but went to another part of the country, and this only after a few years in the original relocation area.

It is this author's estimate that between 8 percent and 13 percent of all relocatees in the two groups from which the samples were drawn have returned to Miami and surrounding areas, but that less than 5 percent can rightly be termed relocation failures. This should not be taken to mean that all relocatees are fully satisfied with their situation in the respective demand areas where they were relocated, though quite a few are. It means only that they do not see any advantage in returning to the original supply area, namely Miami.

It should be emphasized that, from the manpower development point of view, dissatisfaction is not sufficient proof of relocation failure if the people involved have improved their relative position and are no burden to society. Nevertheless, minimizing dissatisfaction is a very important objective of any manpower development program, for dissatisfaction may eventually result in failure. Moreover, if dissatisfaction becomes widespread, would-be relocatees might be discouraged.

An indirect way of estimating the relative incidence of dissatisfaction among the samplers was used. The heads of household were asked to state whether they were considering returning to the Miami area the first time they may have an opportunity. The following was the result:

	Sample 1	Sample 2
yes	8	8
no	40	30
undecided	4	7

The above figures suggest very few were so dissatisfied that they would return to the Miami area at the first opportunity. In addition, those who were so planning were asked to state whether or not they would return even under less favorable conditions than they enjoy now. Almost all stated they would return only under at least similar conditions to those they enjoy presently, but not under less favorable ones.

The performance of the resettlement program for CNR is probably more successful than the above figures suggest, because the Miami area possesses unique attractions related to the particular circumstances of the refugee population. This tends to make CNR prefer the latter over any other location in the United States as a place in which to reside. Be that as it may, it seems safe to conclude that relocation failures, strictly speaking, do not seem to have been a major issue in the resettlement program for CNR.

The experimental relocation program for American families has also done rather well with regard to relocation failures, though perhaps not so well as the program for CNR. In both cases, the reasons most frequently advanced for wanting to return to the original location are very much the same, namely difficulties in adjusting to the new environment, and job dissatisfaction. The problem of adjustment in general should be, at least in theory, a more difficult one for CNR. However, there seem to be two factors working against this hypothesis. First, a very large number of participants in the experimental programs come from economic minorities. This renders the problem of adjustment nearly as difficult as it might be for the CNR. Second, in the case of CNR, quite often the groups and agencies involved have assisted relocatees in adjusting to their new life. Although this has been tried in some of the experimental programs it has been done to a lesser extent.

The issue of retention and failure in relocation is so important that some further exploration was thought to be warranted. An attempt was made to determine if there had been some connection between plans of relocatees to return and certain variables which could be expected to have some bearing on their plans. Plans to return were correlated against current income, change in income after relocation, relative improvement in income (subjective measure), number of years in the United States and age. The first three variables would tend to reflect any financial improvement brought about by relocation. The other two could be expected to influence relocatees' attitudes toward relocation. The longer their residence in this country, the more likely relocatees were to be familiar with its culture. The older a relocatee, the more difficult it is for him to adjust to a new environment. The results of the correlations were as follows:

$$\text{sample 1} \qquad R^2 = .21$$
$$\text{sample 2} \qquad R^2 = .29$$

Neither of the above coefficients of multiple correlation were found to be statistically significant at the 95 percent level of confidence. Furthermore, it was found that one variable alone was responsible for most of the correlation, namely relative income. Relative income was responsible for approximately 80 percent and 70 percent of the above results, respectively. This suggests there has been some tendency for those wanting to return to be among those relocatees who did not think they had improved their financial situation after relocation.

Some further checks for consistency were possible. First, the few who indicated that their children had not adjusted well to the new school system and/or had not been accepted well by other children of the same age were found almost invariably to be among those relocatees who wanted to return. The reverse was not true, however, and the fact that relatively few reported such problems should be interpreted as a very encouraging sign in a society afflicted with racial and group tensions. This is very likely to have contributed to the low rate of relocation failures reported earlier in this section.

A second check was based on what participants thought their future in the demand area to be. A relatively large number of them expressed confidence in their future there; however, in this test a larger number of respondents were undecided. Here too, almost all relocatees who expressed the wish to return were among those who do not think they had a good future in the relocation area.

In general, then, it seems safe to state that, on the average, a desire to return to the Miami area is more often than not associated with either problems of their children's adjustment, or unsatisfactory expectations about their own future, or both.

There is only one check concerning the issue of adaptation which was somewhat inconsistent with the others. Of those relocatees who qualify for naturalization, only about 33 percent in sample 1 and 50 percent in sample 2 have exercised their option. The difference between samples is likely to be partly due to the fact that there are relatively more relocatees in sample 2 who might need to become naturalized to either keep their present job or move to a better one. The fact that in neither sample were there more than 50 percent who have exercised their option might suggest that a considerable number of participants are not yet fully committed, or at least do not feel the need to do so. However, this does not make them relocation failures *per se* from a manpower development point of view.

Major Reasons for Accepting Relocation

It was pointed out earlier that some pressure has been exercised to get CNR to participate in the resettlement program. The fact remains, however, that approximately 50 percent of all CNR have not participated in the program. This suggests then the existence of some viable alternatives. It seems pertinent, therefore, to explore the major reasons for participating in the program. Identifying these reasons may be very valuable in developing this sort of program in the United States.

The reasons given for participating in the program by those in the samples were many. Only those factors which were mentioned most often and given the greatest weight are listed here, namely: a) availability of jobs; b) relatively good pay; c) opportunity to increase family income; d) industrial location; e) better schools for children; f) good housing conditions; g) opportunity to learn English and/or improve skills.

Although at first, some of the factors listed above may appear to be the same, they are not really. For example, jobs may be available, but pay not be good. Or pay may be good, but jobs for women scarce, hence, little opportunity to increase family income.

No major differences were found between the samples with regard to the factors influencing relocation. In most cases, several of the above factors interacted to provide the incentive to relocate. It is likely that any one factor alone may not have proven sufficient to encourage resettlement, for frequently a family takes most of them into account.

It is important to note that better schools and good housing conditions were given considerable weight by the participants in their decision to relocate. This shows that many families are at least as concerned with their children's future as they are with finding a better job. This is very significant to manpower development analysis, for it suggests that better job related conditions might not in themselves be sufficient to stimulate relocation incentive.

Local Assistance

The participation of the federal government in providing financial assistance for relocation purposes was already discussed; however, in many instances it has been the additional assistance furnished by local groups or agencies which has made the difference in convincing families to relocate. In cases where relocation has been automatic, this extra assistance seems to have contributed in influencing some people to stay. This extra assistance has varied, of course, from case to case, particularly from subprogram to subprogram. In some it has been very generous, in others only token. In the case of this study's samples, assistance provided by sponsors has included, on the average: a) an apartment or house (1 to 3 months rent and utilities paid); b) some furniture and other household goods; c) some clothing; d) medical assistance (when required); e) counseling services; f) assistance in establishing credit lines; g) a job.

In addition, a local family has been assigned to help the family to settle down, for example, aid in securing working permits, social security papers, and enrolling children in schools, etc. In some instances, they have even provided temporary transportation, particularly to work. All this is very important to the adjustment of a family in a new location.

The fact that so many hurdles are removed is of much value for the success of the program, for it expedites the incorporation of relocatees into the mainstream of the life of the local community, hence of American life. Proof of the value of this approach is provided, as this author has found, by a greater willingness of relocatees to participate in local, civic, religious and even social organizations when they are so greeted. This should prove invaluable in assisting families to relocate, particularly those from economic minorities.

Some of the groups contacted have indicated some difficulty in finding adequate housing for relocatees. This is, of course, part of the almost nationwide housing crisis and not an exclusive problem of the resettlement program. However, in some of the experimental programs for American families the housing issue had been found to be linked to the problem of discrimination too. This is the sort of obstacle that sponsoring groups in the resettlement program have endeavored to minimize, and with considerable success. So important has this been that in areas where help extended has been limited almost entirely to welfare assistance, the problem of retention appears to have been somewhat critical.

As an indirect check upon the relative importance of this general assistance in persuading people to relocate, participants were asked to state whether or not they would have participated in the resettlement effort in its absence. About 50 percent in both samples were unsure. Another 25 percent replied they would not have relocated. This suggests that the assistance has been an important consideration, if not a deciding one.

Synopsis

The evidence discussed in this section seems to support the view that, in general, the resettlement program has been relatively successful in meeting its objective. This, of course, should not be construed as a blank endorsement of the entire program but only of its potential, in principle, in assisting economic minorities to improve their relative position at a relatively low cost and without conflict with the basic principles of the market system.

Including administration of the resettlement program, the average cost of relocation has been approximately $180 per person, or $720 for a family of four. This average cost, as noted earlier, is rather similar to that incurred in relocating American families. When the cost to private groups is added, the average cost of relocating a family of four has run from $1,000 to $1,500. This does not include the free time devoted to the program by some of the people involved. This private cost applies only to sub-programs, (but not to all sub-programs).

The total cost seems relatively small, particularly that to the government, when the welfare savings, tax revenues, and increase in productivity resulting from the program are taken into account. The above benefits do not even include the improvement in the quality of life, an important intangible which should be expected to result from this sort of effort, particularly if it contributes to the disappearance or prevention of slum-ghetto districts. Though it is beyond measurement, this latter factor certainly plays a role in the decision to allocate resources for this purpose.

It can be concluded, then, that the experience of the resettlement program for CNR has thrown a considerable amount of new light on the actual and potential problems of relocation programs as a major manpower development tool, as well as on possible ways of improving such a mechanism. In particular, it has thrown light on its suitability in assisting economic minorities, not only to increase the marketability of their skills, but also in adding a new dimension to their lives in both its preventive and therapeutic roles.

11 Resettlement: A Concluding Summary

It seems clear that the marketability of the participating CNR's skills has been enhanced greatly, on the average, by relocation, despite the limited knowledge of English possessed by many of them. This strongly suggests the potential contribution of this manpower development tool in matching unemployed and underemployed workers with existing job vacancies, that is, in improving the deployment of the labor force. It has suggested the power of this weapon not only in its own right, but also in cooperation with other manpower development and economic security policies. (The latter aspect was unfortunately not brought out as clearly as it should have been because of particular characteristics of the CNR resettlement program.) This suggests the value of encouraging the policy of relocation itself and also as part of a comprehensive economic security strategy where manpower development is the base.

The experience of the CNR resettlement program has shown that relocation programs can be of value to workers at all levels of skill. Of course, this is not to suggest that all would benefit to the same degree, since they face different problems, particularly at a time when such programs are not part of a rehabilitation in depth mechanism, but of a piecemeal approach. Particularly important has been the finding that low skilled labor was able to find jobs by simply changing labor markets, and with a minimum of other supportive services. This suggests that merely helping low skilled labor to move to a more favorable area may in itself be of some value, though it is hard to say for how long this would be so. Although relocation does not necessarily provide for upward mobility, at least it can prevent the decline of some families into the abyss of poverty and deprivation.

The CNR resettlement program seems to have made abundantly clear that both demand and supply areas can benefit from relocation. This is as it should be, for different grades of labor are complementary as well as competitive in nature. The tendency to treat labor as a homogeneous factor of production has frequently caused this point to be overlooked to a greater or lesser extent. Moreover, the experience of returnees who have been largely rehabilitated prior to their return, suggests that the value of this cross migration does not necessarily end with the first move.

The analysis of this program has also shown the need for greater collaboration between welfare agencies and manpower development agencies, as well as among welfare agencies at the interstate level. During the transitional stage of relocation, welfare or similar assistance may have to be available in the receiving (demand) area in order to encourage workers to relocate. The quantity and quality of the assistance would have to be at least comparable to what they are eligible to receive in their current place of residence.

Included here should be waivers of stringent residence requirements where such requirements exist. Under the present system of semi-autonomous local welfare agencies, collaboration is sometimes difficult, if not impossible to obtain. This reflects, in part, the great diversity in standards and rules among local welfare programs. In addition, although the nation as a whole stands to benefit from such programs, some areas may lose, if only in the short-run, or may not gain as much; therefore, some opposition on those grounds is likely to arise. Yet mutual cooperation is essential, especially if a job offer in the relocation area is not a prerequisite to obtain relocation assistance. This greater collaboration is of utmost importance in any effort to induce economic minorities to relocate.

In the case of the resettlement program for CNR, this problem has been solved in part by the provision of local assistance from federal funds. This is not an unreasonable approach to the extent that the whole nation stands to benefit from this sort of program. The problem however, is likely to become less critical if a guaranteed minimum income is finally established by the federal government, particularly if coupled with further strengthening of the Social Security program, including its further standardization. This would insure participants of a minimum of economic security regardless of their place of residence.

The issue of whether or not a job offer should constitute a prerequisite for obtaining relocation assistance is one that deserves more attention and further research. As matters stand now, the experimental program for American families requires it. It seems appropriate that in the meantime whenever enough evidence exists that labor market conditions are relatively much looser in the would-be relocation area than they are in the supply area, no job requirement should be necessary to obtain relocation assistance, at least not for economic minorities.

To the extent that a comprehensive program of labor mobility is established and participants are expected to pay in the long-run for such assistance in accordance with the benefits they receive, the principle of a job requirement should be dropped. Sometimes, it is possible to anticipate declines in some labor markets and expansion in others, for example, when an industry that is the major source of employment in a given labor market is considering major technological changes that would cause large scale displacement, labor mobility assistance can speed up the painful adjustment process that is likely to ensue. This would be greatly aided by the current development of a job bank, labor market analysis studies, and a communication network among labor markets.

This study of the resettlement program for CNR also suggests the pivotal role played by religious, civic, and other private groups in removing many of the obstacles that may render relocation programs less effective, especially programs whose major target is economic minorities. The process of incorporating economic minority groups into the mainstream of American life has to begin at the local level if it is going to have a relatively good chance of being successful. When participants in relocation schemes feel they are being left out or discriminated against there is inevitably a greater tendency to return to the area of origin. In the case of many economic minority groups this is quite often a slum and/or ghetto. The workers assisting relocatees in the experimental programs for American families are, for the most part, devoted and well-meaning people, but they are not well equipped to overcome many of the barriers facing economic minorities; therefore, they should explore ways of obtaining the full cooperation of these private groups. This, of course, is by no means a simple task. The CAA, if successful in attracting local cooperation could conceivably be of value in this respect. Yet, it is hard to envision whether or not mobility programs are of interest to them.

The experience of the experimental program for American families has suggested that relocation programs can make other manpower development weapons more effective. Of particular interest in this respect is its potential to increase the effectiveness of retraining programs. Combined, they might be able to provide some minimum of upward mobility, which is especially important to economic minorities. In the program for CNR, this link, though present, has not been fully exploited; but even English classes have proved of great value in quite a few instances.

In extending the possibilities suggested by the experience of the CNR resettlement program to other economic minority groups, this author is aware of possible differences between this group and other economic minorities. As pointed out earlier, economic minorities are far from a homogeneous group. Some are culturally and economically disadvantaged, some only the latter. Still others have been economic minorities for several generations which in itself is likely to have added to the handicaps they face. Moreover, new groups may become part of this family in the absence of adequate means to prevent this. All these differences, as they exist, must be taken into account in devising comprehensive mobility programs as part of any major manpower development effort. Nevertheless, CNRs have been—and many still are—members of this population of economic minorities and they do share some of the major characteristics of this family, including the fact that they are socially and politically a minority group. They have a tendency to band together—something which in the face of economic insecurity may give rise to the development of slum-ghetto type districts.

The resettlement program has provided ample evidence of the potential of this approach in helping to prevent CNR from becoming more like other culturally deprived economic minorities. This has been accomplished by tackling the problem at an early stage and at its very heart. The program has provided only limited evidence, however, of its potential as a therapeutic device, that is in helping those who have been economically and sometimes culturally disadvantaged for many years. This is likely to be a greater challenge. However, the evidence provided by the experimental program for American families together with whatever experience the CNR resettlement program may have provided does support the view that this mechanism should prove to be a powerful therapeutic weapon as well as a preventive one.

The most difficult problem, apart from discrimination, that seems to exist in devising and implementing relocation programs for economic minorities is that of finding jobs suitable to their skills. The fact that many of the low skill workers among the CNR who have participated in the program have found relatively good jobs suggests that it may yet be possible to help some members of the economic minority family with the provision of mobility assistance. However, a lasting solution in the case of economic minorities would require rehabilitation in depth, including, whenever necessary, mobility assistance; for once rehabilitated, they might still need to migrate. Of course, the amount of rehabilitation will tend to vary with the problems of the particular individual or group involved. However, the experience gained from current programs is invaluable in assisting to find what factors seem to be more important in motivating or discouraging people to participate and must be exploited to the fullest to create the right environment for these programs to work. For example, many of the CNR who have participated in the mobility program had a strong motivation to become independent for many reasons, which may help in finding the right blend to encourage the labor mobility of other groups.

With regard to mobility programs in general, the conclusion here is that they have great potential in bringing about an orderly redistribution of population with a minimum of friction and in a manner which is quite consistent with the underlying philosophy of this study, that is, the strengthening of the effectiveness of the market mechanism in more nearly optimizing the allocation of scarce economic resources. Such programs can contribute greatly then to the gradual, but steady, elimination of slums which is particularly important in the case of economic minorities. It is not this author's intention to suggest that this is the only road open, but merely to suggest that it is certainly a workable one. This is true, regardless of the final approach chosen to solve the challenge posed by economic insecurity.

While Congress has not yet committed itself to support mobility programs, it is hoped that this attitude will soon undergo some change, because, it is incumbent upon our political leadership to sponsor policies that will strengthen our economic system, and mobility programs do show considerable promise of doing so.

Appendix

Table A-1
Change in Population by Age Group[a]

Age	Number Change (in thousands)				Percentage Change			
	1950-60	1960-70	1970-80	1980-90	1950-60	1960-70	1970-80	1980-90
Total	28,413	24,713	27,015	33,907	18.7	13.7	13.2	14.6
Under 16 years	15,737	4,163	2,215	15,076	36.5	7.1	3.6	23.1
16 to 19	2,156	4,384	1,810	– 846	25.2	41.0	12.0	– 5.0
20 to 24	– 564	6,060	3,735	– 2,653	– 4.8	54.5	21.7	–12.7
25 to 34	–1,125	2,432	11,436	5,412	– 4.7	10.6	45.1	14.7
35 to 44	2,586	–1,180	2,480	11,240	12.0	– 4.9	10.8	44.0
45 to 54	3,128	2,808	–1,037	2,465	17.9	13.6	– 4.4	11.0
55 to 64	2,231	2,877	2,676	– 862	16.7	18.4	14.5	– 4.1
65 and over	4,261	3,170	3,664	4,075	34.4	19.0	18.5	17.3

[a]Projections are based on intermediate fertility assumptions.

Source: *Manpower Report of the President*, 1971.

Table A-2
Labor Force by Age Group and Sex

Age	(In thousands)					Percentage Change			
	1950	1960	1970	1980a	1985a	1950-60	1960-70	1970-80	1980-85
Male									
16 years and over	45,446	48,933	54,343	63,612	67,718	7.7	11.1	17.1	6.4
16 to 24	8,045	8,101	11,773	13,690	13,179	.6	45.3	16.3	− 3.8
25 to 34	11,044	10,940	11,974	17,815	19,601	− .9	9.5	48.8	10.0
35 to 44	9,952	11,454	10,818	12,086	15,020	15.1	− 5.6	11.7	24.2
45 to 64	13,952	16,013	17,614	17,931	17,773	14.8	10.0	1.8	− .9
65 and over	2,453	2,425	2,164	2,090	2,145	−1.1	−10.8	− 3.4	2.6
Female									
16 years and over	18,412	23,171	31,560	37,115	39,438	25.8	36.2	17.6	6.2
16 to 24	4,395	4,619	8,143	9,440	9,063	5.1	76.3	15.9	− 4.0
25 to 34	4,101	4,159	5,704	8,427	9,431	1.4	37.1	47.7	11.9
35 to 44	4,166	5,325	5,971	6,708	8,397	27.8	12.1	12.3	25.1
45 to 64	5,167	8,114	10,686	11,362	11,289	57.0	31.7	6.3	− .7
65 and over	584	954	1,056	1,178	1,258	63.4	10.7	11.6	6.7

aProjected figures.

Source: *Manpower Report of the President, 1971.*

Table A-3
Labor Force Participation Rates by Age Group and Sex

Age	1950	1960	1970	1980[a]	1985[a]
Male					
16 years and over	86.8	82.4	79.2	79.2	79.6
16 to 19	65.5	58.6	57.5	56.7	56.4
20 to 24	89.1	88.9	85.1	83.0	82.5
25 to 34	96.2	96.4	95.0	96.0	96.0
35 to 44	97.6	96.4	95.7	96.1	96.1
45 to 54	95.8	94.3	92.9	94.0	94.0
55 to 64	86.9	85.2	81.5	80.5	79.9
65 and over	45.8	32.2	25.1	22.0	21.1
Female					
16 years and over	33.9	37.1	42.8	43.0	43.2
16 to 19	40.9	39.1	43.7	41.5	41.0
20 to 24	46.1	46.1	57.5	57.6	57.7
25 to 34	34.0	35.8	44.8	45.7	46.5
35 to 44	39.1	43.1	50.9	52.4	53.3
45 to 54	38.0	49.3	54.0	54.8	55.2
55 to 64	27.0	36.7	42.5	45.2	45.0
65 and over	9.7	10.5	9.2	8.7	8.5

[a]Projected figures.
Source: *Manpower Report of the President*, 1971.

Table A-4
Percentage Change in Population and Labor Force by Major Region

	Population		Labor Force	
	1960-70	1970-80[a]	1960-70	1970-80[a]
United States	16.8	16.9	21.1	18.3
New England	12.6	14.5	15.7	14.5
Middle Atlantic	12.6	12.3	14.7	12.1
East North Central	12.8	16.2	16.9	18.0
West North Central	8.0	12.2	13.6	15.0
South Atlantic	22.0	19.5	26.3	20.1
East South Central	14.5	13.5	21.3	17.1
West South Central	18.3	16.8	23.7	20.4
Mountain	30.1	24.2	38.5	27.3
Pacific	28.5	24.7	33.4	25.6

[a]Projected figures.
Source: *Manpower Report of the President*, 1971.

Table A-5
Workers in Non-agricultural Employment on Voluntary Part-time Schedules by Age Group and Sex

Age	(In thousands)		
	1957[a]	1960[a]	1970[b]
Male			
Total	34.5	33.9	32.2
under 18 years	14.2	13.2	9.2
18 to 24	6.3	6.7	11.0
25 to 44	3.5	3.3	3.0
45 to 64	4.4	4.1	3.3
65 and over	6.1	6.6	5.8
Female			
Total	65.5	66.1	67.8
under 18 years	10.1	10.2	8.2
18 to 24	6.4	6.7	12.2
25 to 44	24.1	23.8	23.9
45 to 64	20.3	20.2	19.1
65 and over	4.6	5.2	4.4

[a]Persons 14 years of age and over.
[b]Persons 16 years of age and over.
Source: *Manpower Report of the President*, 1971 and *Statistical Supplement* to the *Manpower Report of the President*, 1965.

Table A-6
Median Years of School Completed, for Persons 18 Years of Age and Over by Sex and Race

	1940[a]	1952	1962	1970	1980[b]
Both sexes	9.1	10.9	12.0	12.4	12.5
White		11.4	12.2	12.4	
Non-white		7.6	9.6	11.7	
Male	7.7	10.4	12.0	12.4	12.5
White		10.8	12.1	12.4	
Non-white		7.2	9.0	11.1	
Female	11.0	12.0	12.2	12.4	12.5
White		12.1	12.3	12.5	
Non-white		8.1	10.5	12.1	

[a]Special Labor Force Report No. 92, U.S. Department of Labor, 1968.
[b]Projected figures for persons 25 years of age and over.
Source: *Manpower Report of the President*, 1971.

Table A-7

Percent Distribution of the Labor Force 18 Years Old and Over by Years of School Completed and Race

	Both Sexes				Whites				Non-whites			
	1952	1962	1970	1980[a]	1952	1962	1970	1980[a]	1952	1962	1970	1980[a]
Less than 5 years	7.3	4.6	2.4	1.8	5.2	3.3	1.8	1.3	26.7	15.4	7.4	5.4
5 to 8 years	30.2	22.4	15.1	10.1	29.3	21.4	14.4	9.5	38.7	29.8	20.6	15.4
9 to 11 years	18.5	19.3	17.3	16.8	18.7	18.8	16.4	16.0	15.9	23.2	24.7	23.2
12 years	26.6	32.1	39.0	42.4	28.3	33.5	40.0	43.2	10.8	21.0	31.0	36.3
1 to 3 years of college	8.3	10.7	13.3	12.0	8.8	11.3	13.9	12.4	3.7	5.7	9.0	9.3
4 years or more of college	7.9	11.0	12.9	16.9	8.5	11.8	13.6	17.8	2.6	4.8	7.4	10.5

[a]Projected figures for persons 25 years of age and over.

Source: *Manpower Report of the President, 1971.*

Table A-8

Percent Distribution of Personal Consumption Expenditures and Projected Average Annual Rates of Change by Major Type of Goods and Services.[a]

	1950	1957	1965	1968	Projected 1980 Services	Projected 1980 Durables	Annual Rate of Change 1965-80 Services	Annual Rate of Change 1965-80 Durables
Durable goods	15.9	12.5	14.6	15.5	15.2	16.5	4.2	4.8
Automobiles and parts	6.9	5.6	6.6	6.9	5.8	6.3	2.8	3.5
Furniture and household Equipment	7.4	5.2	6.0	6.4	7.0	7.5	5.1	5.6
Other	1.6	1.7	2.0	2.3	2.5	2.7	5.3	5.8
Nondurable goods	51.3	47.4	44.3	43.0	38.3	37.7	3.4	3.1
Food and beverages	28.2	26.0	22.8	21.4	19.0	18.7	3.3	3.0
Clothing and shoes	10.3	8.7	8.6	8.6	7.1	7.0	2.7	2.4
Gasoline and oil	2.8	3.5	3.5	3.6	2.9	2.8	2.5	2.3
Other	10.0	9.2	9.4	9.3	9.3	9.2	4.4	4.1
Services	32.8	40.1	41.1	41.5	46.4	45.8	5.3	5.1
Housing	11.2	13.3	14.3	14.4	17.3	17.3	6.0	5.9
Household operation	4.9	5.6	5.7	5.8	6.1	6.0	4.8	4.5
Transportation	3.3	3.5	3.0	3.0	3.1	3.0	4.6	4.3
Other	13.4	17.7	18.2	18.3	19.8	19.4	5.1	4.7

[a]Projected figures are based on an assumed unemployment rate of 4 percent.

Source: *The U.S. Economy in 1980*, Bulletin 1673, U.S. Department of Labor, 1970 and *Economic Report of the President*, 1971.

Table A-9

Average Annual Rates of Change of Domestic Output by Major Industry Group

	1947-57	1957-65	Projected 1965-80[a] Services	Projected 1965-80[a] Durables
Agriculture, forestry and fisheries	1.4	2.1	2.9	2.7
Mining	2.5	1.7	3.4	3.4
Manufacturing	3.5	4.1	4.2	4.4
Communications and public utilities	8.6	6.0	6.6	6.5
Finance, insurance and real estate	5.0	5.2	4.8	4.6
Services and miscellaneous	3.5	4.6	5.5	5.3
Government enterprises	3.3	5.3	5.3	5.1
Federal government	4.9	6.1	5.0	4.9
State and local	2.3	4.8	5.4	5.3

[a]Projected figures are based on an assumed unemployment rate of 4 percent.

Source: *The U.S. Economy in 1980*, Bulletin 1673, U.S. Department of Labor, 1970 and *Economic Report of the President*, 1971.

Table A-10
Percent Distribution of Employment by Major Occupational Groups

	1950[a]	1960[b]	1970[b]	1980[c]
White collar	37.5	43.4	48.3	50.8
Professional and technical	7.5	11.4	14.2	16.3
Managers, officials, proprietors	10.8	10.7	10.5	10.0
Clerical	12.8	14.8	17.4	18.2
Sales	6.4	6.4	6.2	6.3
Blue collar	39.1	36.6	35.3	32.7
Craftsmen, foremen	12.9	13.0	12.9	12.8
Operatives	20.3	18.2	17.7	16.2
Nonfarm labor	5.9	5.4	4.7	3.7
Service	11.0	12.2	12.4	13.8
Private household	3.2	3.0	2.0	–
Other services	7.8	9.2	10.4	–
Farm	12.5	7.9	4.0	2.7
Farmers and managers	7.4	4.2	2.2	–
Farm laborers and foremen	5.1	3.3	1.7	–

[a]Persons 14 years of age and over.
[b]Persons 16 years of age and over.
[c]Projected figures.
Source: *Manpower Report of the President*, 1971 and *Statistical Supplement to the Manpower Report of the President*, 1965.

Table A-11

Percent Distribution of Employment in the Non-agricultural Sector by Type of Industry

	1950	1960	1968	1980[a]
Mining	2.0	1.3	.9	.6
Contract construction	5.0	5.3	4.8	5.3
Manufacturing	34.0	31.0	29.1	25.3
Durables	18.0	17.4	17.1	15.0
Nondurables	16.0	13.5	12.0	10.3
Transportation and public utilities	9.0	1.4	6.4	5.5
Transportation	4.0	4.7	3.9	3.3
Communications	4.0	1.5	1.5	1.3
Electric, gas, and sanitary services	1.0	1.1	1.0	.8
Trade	21.0	21.0	20.8	20.4
Wholesale	6.0	5.5	5.3	5.3
Retail	15.0	15.5	15.4	15.0
Finance, insurance, and real estate	4.0	4.9	5.0	4.9
Service and miscellaneous	12.0	13.7	15.6	18.6
Government	13.0	15.4	17.5	19.4
Federal	4.0	4.2	4.0	3.5
State and local	9.0	11.2	13.4	15.9

[a]Projected figures.

Source: *Manpower Report of the President*, 1971 and *Statistical Supplement to the Manpower Report of the President*, 1965.

Table A-12

Unemployment Rates of Persons 16 Years of Age and Over by Race, Sex, and Age Group

	1950				1960				1970			
	M-W	F-W	M-NW	F-NW	M-W	F-W	M-NW	F-NW	M-W	F-W	M-NW	F-NW
16 years and over	4.7	5.3	9.4	8.4	4.8	5.3	10.7	9.4	4.0	5.4	7.3	9.3
16 and 17	13.4	13.8	21.1	17.6	14.6	14.5	22.7	25.7	15.7	15.3	27.8	36.9
18 and 19	11.7	9.4	17.7	14.1	13.5	11.5	25.1	24.5	12.0	11.9	23.1	32.9
20 to 24	7.7	6.1	12.6	13.0	8.3	7.2	13.1	15.3	7.8	6.9	12.6	15.0
25 to 34	3.9	5.2	10.0	9.1	4.1	5.7	10.7	9.1	3.1	5.3	6.1	7.9
35 to 44	3.2	4.0	7.9	6.6	3.3	4.2	8.2	8.6	2.3	4.3	3.9	4.8
45 to 54	3.7	4.3	7.4	5.9	3.6	4.0	8.5	5.7	2.3	3.4	3.8	4.0
55 to 64	4.7	4.3	8.0	4.8	4.1	3.3	9.5	4.3	2.7	2.6	3.4	3.2
65 and over	4.6	3.1	7.0	5.7	4.0	2.8	6.3	4.1	3.2	3.3	3.8	1.9
14 and 15	5.8	8.0	10.8	–	8.1	6.3	13.3	–	10.1	7.4	29.0	30.9

M-W: male white, F-W: female white, M-NW: male nonwhite, F-NW: female nonwhite

Source: *Manpower Report of the President*, 1971.

Table A-13
Unemployment Rates of Persons 16 Years of Age and Over by Major Occupational Group

	1958	1960	1965	1970
Total unemployment	6.8	5.5	4.5	4.9
White collar	3.1	2.7	2.3	2.8
Professional and technical	2.0	1.7	1.5	2.0
Managers and officials	1.7	1.4	1.1	1.3
Clerical	4.4	3.8	3.3	4.0
Sales	4.1	3.8	3.4	3.9
Blue collar	10.2	7.8	5.3	6.2
Craftsmen and foremen	6.8	5.3	3.6	3.8
Operatives	11.0	8.0	5.5	7.1
Nonfarm labor	15.0	12.6	8.6	9.5
Service	6.9	5.8	5.3	5.3
Private household	5.6	5.3	4.7	4.2
Other services	7.4	6.0	5.5	5.5
Farmers and farm laborers	3.2	2.7	2.6	2.6

Source: *Manpower Report of the President*, 1971.

Table A-14
Unemployment Rates for a Selected Number of States

	1960	1965	1970
Alabama	6.3	4.4	4.8
Alaska	8.0	8.6	10.2
California	5.8	5.9	6.0
Illinois	4.2	3.3	3.9
Louisiana	6.5	4.9	6.2
Massachusetts	5.1	4.9	5.2
Michigan	6.7	3.9	7.0
New Mexico	5.4	5.5	6.3
New York	5.6	4.4	4.6
Virginia	4.2	3.0	3.1
Wyoming	4.4	4.4	4.3

Source: *Manpower Report of the President*, 1971.

Table A-15
An Example of the Effect of Taxing Personal Income Below the Break-even
Level of Income in Guaranteed Minimum Income Schemes

(1) Basic Allowance	(2) Offsetting Tax Rate %	(3) Personal Income Tax Rate %	(4) Income	(5) Personal Income Taxes (4) x (3)	(6) Offsetting Tax (4) x (2)	(7) Net Benefits (1)–(6)	(8) Disposable Income (4)–(5)+(7)
$2,400	50	14	0	0	0	$2,400	$2,400
			$1,000	$140	$ 500	$1,900	$2,760
			$2,000	$280	$1,000	$1,400	$3,120
$2,400	64	0	0	0	0	$2,400	$2,400
			$1,000	0	$ 640	$1,760	$2,760
			$2,000	0	$1,280	$1,120	$3,120

Source: Edward Moscovitch, "Income Supplements–How High Should They Be," in the *New England Economic Review*, Federal Reserve Bank of Boston.

Table A-16
Percent Distribution of Enrollment in Federally Aided Vocational-Technical
Education by Occupation

	1964	1969
Agriculture	18.8	10.7
Distributive	7.3	7.1
Health	1.3	2.2
Home economics	44.3	30.7
Office	–	23.0
Technical	4.8	3.9
Trades and industry	23.4	21.6
Other	–	.9

Source: *Manpower Report of the President*, 1971.

Table A-17
Migration Rates (1955 to 1960 of Family Heads 25 Years Old and Over by Age, Race, and Family Income

Income[a]	Age Group				
	25 to 29	30 to 34	35 to 44	45 to 64	65 and Over
Total	34.9	25.4	17.3	9.3	7.1
Under $1,000	24.3	19.8	14.8	10.1	6.2
1,000 to 1,999	29.1	21.0	15.6	10.0	7.2
2,000 to 2,999	33.1	22.3	15.5	10.0	8.6
3,000 to 3,999	33.8	24.8	16.4	9.6	8.2
4,000 to 4,999	34.3	24.1	16.1	8.9	7.2
5,000 to 5,999	34.4	23.2	15.2	8.6	6.5
6,000 to 6,999	36.3	24.6	16.1	8.8	6.4
7,000 to 9,999	37.3	27.7	18.0	9.2	5.8
10,000 to 14,999	38.5	30.5	21.1	9.6	5.5
15,000 and over	35.3	29.2	19.2	10.0	5.3
Non-white	20.2	13.0	8.1	4.6	2.8
Under $1,000	14.8	11.9	9.6	5.4	3.5
1,000 to 1,999	18.3	12.0	8.7	5.2	2.6
2,000 to 2,999	20.9	12.9	8.5	4.9	2.5
3,000 to 3,999	20.8	14.1	8.3	4.6	3.0
4,000 to 4,999	21.7	13.3	7.3	3.9	2.2
5,000 to 5,999	21.5	12.3	7.4	3.6	2.7
6,000 to 6,999	20.3	12.0	8.0	4.2	2.3
7,000 to 9,999	20.0	13.2	7.4	4.3	1.7
10,000 to 14,999	19.4	13.7	8.7	4.3	2.1
15,000 and over	22.5	18.1	12.0	4.0	1.6

[a]1959 income.

Source: *Statistical Tables on Manpower, Manpower Report of the President*, 1965.

Notes

Notes

Notes to Introduction

1. Fred M. Hechniger, *The New York Times Book Review* (New York: 1966).
2. For an analysis of the concept of poverty bands, see Oscar Ornati, *Poverty Amid Affluence* (New York: The Twentieth Century Fund, 1966), p. *11*.

Notes to Chapter 1

1. See the statistical appendix of the Manpower Report of the President, 1971 (Washington, D.C.: U.S. Government Printing Office).
2. D.F. Johnson and G.R. Methee, "Labor Force Projections by State, 1970 and 1980," *Special Labor Force Report No. 74* (Washington, D.C.: U.S. Department of Labor, October 1966), pp. 1098-1104. Also, Manpower Report of the President, 1971 (Washington, D.C.: U.S. Government Printing Office).
3. Seymour L. Wolfbein, *Employment and Unemployment in the U.S.* (Chicago: Science Research Associates, 1964), p. 121.
4. See the Manpower Report of the President, 1971.
5. For one of the best expositions of this subject see, T.W. Schultz, *Investment in Human Capital* (New York: Free Press, 1971).
6. Ibid., pp. 123-126.
7. Economic Report of the President, 1971.
8. Ibid.
9. R.E. Kutscher and E.E. Jacobs, "Factors Affecting Changes in Industry Employment," *Monthly Labor Review*, Reprint No. 2529 (Washington, D.C.: U.S. Department of Labor, April 1967), pp. 6-12.
10. For an excellent treatment of this issue see, J. Rezler, *Automation and Industrial Labor* (New York, Random House, 1969).
11. For a detailed discussion of changes in the location of production see, Victor R. Fuchs, *Changes in the Location of Manufacturing in the United States Since 1929* (New Haven: Yale University Press, 1962).
12. Manpower Report of the President, 1971.
13. For a detailed analysis of this change in the pace of automation as well as its timing see, E. Gilpatric, *Structural Unemployment and Aggregate Demand* (Baltimore: John Hopkins Press, 1966).

Notes to Chapter 2

1. Robert L. Heilbroner, *The Limits of American Capitalism* (New York: Harper Torchbook, Harper and Row, 1966), and John K. Galbraith, *The New Industrial State* (Boston: Houghton Mifflin and Co., 1967).

156

2. For a discussion of how these projections are made see, *Manpower Directions New York State 1965-1975, Technical Supplement* (New York: New York State Department of Labor, 1968).

3. See, for example, Richard A. Lester, "Effectiveness of Factory Labor: South-North Comparisons," *Journal of Political Economy* (February 1946), vol. 54, pp. 60-75.

Notes to Chapter 3

1. See, A.W. Phillips, "The Relation Between Unemployment and the Rate of Change of Money Wage Rates in the United Kingdom 1861-1957," *Economica* (1958), vol. 25, pp. 283-299. Also, W.G. Bowen, *Wage Behavior in the Post-War Period* (Princeton: Princeton University, 1960).

2. Milton Friedman, "The Role of Monetary Policy," *American Economic Review* (March 1968), vol. LVIII, pp. 1-17.

3. R. Meidner, "Active Manpower Policy and the Inflation-Unemployment Dilemma," *The Swedish Journal of Economics* (September 1969), vol. 71.

4. M.S. Cohen, "The Direct Effect of Federal Manpower Programs in Reducing Unemployment," *The Journal of Human Resources* (Fall 1969), vol. 4, pp. 491-507.

5. Oscar Ornati, Spatial Distribution of Urban Poverty, in *Power Poverty and Urban Policy*, vol. 2, W. Blomberg, Jr., and J.J. Schmandt, eds. (Beverly Hills: Sage Publications, Inc., 1968), p. 58.

6. See, Schultz, op. cit.

7. F. Welch, "Education in Production," *Journal of Political Economy* (January-February 1970), vol. 78, pp. 35-59.

8. For an explanation of frictional unemployment see, B.R. Bergman and D.E. Kaun, *Structural Unemployment in the U.S.*, The Brookings Institution for the U.S. Department of Commerce (Washington, D.C.: U.S. Government Printing Office), pp. 2-3.

9. For a discussion of this interaction see Gilpatric, op. cit., pp. 13-14.

10. Richard A. Lester, *Manpower Planning in a Free Society* (Princeton: Princeton University Press, 1966), p. 131.

11. For some estimates see, Bergman and Kaun, op. cit., pp. 105-108, and Gilpatric, op. cit., pp. 203-214.

Notes to Chapter 4

1. Manpower Report of the President, 1971.

2. See G.F. Bloom and H.R. Northrup, *Economics of Labor Relations* (Homewood: Richard D. Irwin, 1969), p. 162.

3. See the 1968 Supplement MC 58(1)-9 to the U.S. Census of Manufacturers for some evidence supporting this view.

4. For an analysis of this influence see, Duncan M. MacIntyre, *Public Assistance, Too Much or Too Little* (Ithaca: N.Y. State School of Industrial and Labor Relations, 1964), pp. 8-25.

5. *The Wall Street Journal*, June 6, 1971. In total some 57 million people were reported receiving some kind of income from the government, not counting public employees.

6. C. Green, *Negative Taxes and the Poverty Problem* (Washington, D.C.: The Brookings Institution, 1967), p. 16.

7. H.J. Aaron, "Income Transfer Programs," p. 53 in Perspective on Poverty, *Monthly Labor Review*, February. Reprint No. 2604 (Washington, D.C.: U.S. Department of Labor, February 1969), pp. 32-62.

8. For an attempt to consider this problem, see D.H. Greenberg and M. Koster, "The Impact of Income Maintenance Programs on Hours of Work and Incomes of the Working Poor: Some Empirical Results," *Industrial Relations Research Association*, Annual Proceedings, (1970), pp. 341-351.

9. Aaron, op. cit., p. 51.

10. For an analytical exposition of this problem see, Richard Perlman, *Labor Theory* (New York: John Wiley and Sons, Inc., 1969), pp. 63-76.

11. *The Potential for Work Among Welfare Parents* (Washington, D.C.: Manpower Research Monograph No. 12, Manpower Administration, U.S. Department of Labor, 1969).

12. J. Mooney, "Urban Poverty and Labor Force Participation," *American Economic Review* (March 1967), vol. LVII, pp. 104-119.

13. For a detailed discussion of the cost of alternative programs and levels of assistance see Edward Moscovitch, "Income Supplements: How High Should They Be," *The New England Economic Review* (Federal Reserve Bank of Boston, January-February 1971), pp. 5-39.

14. See, J.L. Freund, "Income Maintenance Programs: Spending the Benefits," *Business Review* (Federal Reserve Bank of Philadelphia, April 1971), pp. 15-25.

15. *Improving the Public Welfare System*, Committee for Economic Development (April 1970), p. 20.

16. *Associated Press*, June 13, 1971.

17. *New York Times News Service*, June 8, 1971.

18. Manpower Report of the President, 1971.

19. *New York Times News Service*, June 15, 1971.

Notes to Chapter 5

1. Eli Ginzberg, *Manpower Agenda for America* (New York: McGraw-Hill Book Company, 1968), p. 73.

2. Dorothy K. Newman, "Changing Attitudes About the Poor," in *Perspective on Poverty*, op. cit., pp. 32-36.

3. Ornati, op. cit.

4. *Poverty in the United States*, Committee on Education and Labor, House of Representatives, 88th Congress (Washington, D.C.: Government Printing Office, 1964).

5. See Susan Holland, "Adult Men Not in the Labor Force," *Special Labor Force Report No. 79* (Washington, D.C.: U.S. Department of Labor, March 1967), pp. 5-15.

6. See Vera G. Perrella and Elizabeth Waldman, "Out-of-School Youth— Two Years Later," *Special Labor Force Report No. 71* (Washington, D.C.: U.S. Department of Labor, August 1966), pp. 860-866.

7. James R. Bright, The Relationship of Increasing Automation to Skill Requirements, in *Manpower Problems and Policies: Full Employment and Opportunity for All*, John A. Delehanty, ed. (Scranton: International Textbook Co., 1969), p. 174.

8. Jerry M. Rosenberg, *Automation, Manpower and Education* (New York: Random House, 1966), p. 16.

9. John A. Brittain, "The Incidence of Social Security Payroll Taxes," *American Economic Review* (March 1971), vol. LXI, pp. 110-125.

10. W. Lee Hansen, "Income Distribution Effects of Higher Education," *American Economic Review*, Papers and Proceedings (May 1970), vol. LX, pp. 335-340.

Notes to Chapter 6

1. See, the Manpower Report of the President, 1971.

2. For a detailed account of the legislative evolution of the MDTA see, Garth Mangum, *MDTA Foundation of Federal Manpower Policy* (Baltimore: The Johns Hopkins Press, 1968).

3. See, the 1966 Report of the Secretary of Labor on Manpower Research and Training under the MDTA (Washington, D.C.: U.S. Department of Labor, 1966).

4. *Job Development for the Hard-to-Employ*, MDTA Experimental and Demonstration Finding No. 4 (Washington, D.C.: U.S. Department of Labor, Manpower Administration, June 1968).

5. See, *Review of Economic Opportunity Programs*, Report to the Congress of the U.S. (Washington, D.C.: U.S. Government Printing Office, March 1969).

6. See, J.E. Gordon, *Testing, Counseling and Supportive Services*, in Breakthrough for Disadvantaged Youth (Washington, D.C.: U.S. Department of Labor, 1969).

7. Garth L. Mangum, *The Emergence of Manpower Policy* (New York: Holt, Rinehart, and Winston, Inc., 1969), p. 89.

Notes to Chapter 8

1. See, J.E. Parker and J.F. Burton, Jr., "Voluntary Labor Mobility in the U.S. Manufacturing Sector," *Industrial Relations Research Association*, Proceedings (1967), pp. 61-70.

2. Michael J. Brennan, *Regional Labor and Capital Migration*, Contract No. C-325-65 (May 31, 1967), p. 73.

3. L. Reynolds, *The Structure of Labor Markets* (New York: Harper and Brothers, 1951), p. 215.

4. Samuel Saben, "Occupational Mobility of Employed Workers," *Special Labor Force Report No. 84* (Washington, D.C.: U.S. Bureau of Labor Statistics, June 1967), pp. 31-38.

5. *The Geographic Mobility of Labor: A Summary Report*, U.S. Department of Commerce (Washington, D.C.: U.S. Government Printing Office, 1964), p. 7.

6. Ibid., pp. 7-8.

7. Reports and Inquiries: Labour Mobility in the United States," *International Labor Review*, March 1959, vol. 79, pp. 296-314.

8. The Geographic Mobility, op. cit., p. 13.

9. For a detailed discussion of this problem, see J.B. Lansing and E. Mueller, *The Geographic Mobility of Labor* (Ann Arbor: Institute for Social Research, University of Michigan, 1967).

10. R.L. Raimon, "Interstate Migration and Wage Theory," *Review of Economics and Statistics* (1962), vol. 44, pp. 428-438.

11. *Statistical Tables on Manpower* (Washington, D.C.: U.S. Department of Labor, March 1965).

Notes to Chapter 9

1. L. Sjaastad, "The Costs and Returns of Human Migration," *Journal of Political Economy*, Supplement (October 1962), vol. 70, pp. 80-93.

2. E.C. and K.S. Koziara, "Development of Relocation Allowances as Manpower Policy," *Industrial and Labor Relations Review* (October 1966), vol. 20, pp. 66-75.

3. For a detailed treatment of some of the most important factors affecting migration see, G.L. Palmer, *Labor Mobility in Six Cities* (New York: Social Science Research Council, 1954). For a more recent treatment of the subject see, Lansing and Mueller, op. cit.

4. See, A. Freedman, "Labor Mobility Projects for the Unemployed," *Monthly Labor Review*, U.S. Department of Labor (June 1968), vol. 91, pp. 56-62.

5. Ibid.

6. See, W. Mirengoff, *Planned Relocation in the U.S.*, p. 240, in *Symposium on the Role of Worker Relocation in an Active Manpower Policy*, April 9-11, 1969 (Washington, D.C.: U.S. Department of Labor). Conducted by the International Manpower Institute.

7. Manpower Report of the President, 1971.

8. See. C. Davis, *Selected Worker Relocation Projects in the United States*, p. 78 in Symposium, op. cit.

Notes to Chapter 10

1. The F test serves to compare the variance of two samples. For a detailed discussion of this test see, W.L. Hays and R.L. Winkler, *Statistics: Probability, Inference, and Decision* (New York: Holt, Rinehart and Winston, 1970).

2. *The Cuban Refugee in the Public Schools of Dade County*, Reports 6, 7 and 8 (Miami: Dade County School Board, March 1970), pp. 3-4.

About the Author

Eloy R. Mestre was born in Havana, Cuba in 1939. He did his undergraduate work at the University of Havana and graduate work at the New School for Social Research in New York City where he received an M.A. in 1964 and Ph.D. in 1969. Mr. Mestre taught at Georgia Southern College and for the past four years has taught labor economics and macroeconomics at State University College at Oneonta where he is professor of Economics. He will soon join the staff of the Organization of American States as Senior Economist.